Help Wanted

Help Wanted

How to Find and Keep Talent in a Forever-Tight Labor Market

Jerry Rubin and Steven L. Dawson

The MIT Press
Cambridge, Massachusetts
London, England

The MIT Press
Massachusetts Institute of Technology
77 Massachusetts Avenue
Cambridge, MA 02139
mitpress.mit.edu

The MIT Press would like to thank the anonymous peer reviewers who provided comments on drafts of this book. The generous work of academic experts is essential for establishing the authority and quality of our publications. We acknowledge with gratitude the contributions of these otherwise uncredited readers.

This book was set in ITC Stone Serif Std and ITC Stone Sans Std by New Best-set Typesetters Ltd. Printed and bound in the United States of America.

Library of Congress Cataloging-in-Publication Data is available.

ISBN: 978-0-262-05439-3

10 9 8 7 6 5 4 3 2 1

EU Authorised Representative: Easy Access System Europe, Mustamäe tee 50, 10621 Tallinn, Estonia | Email: gpsr.requests@easproject.com

We dedicate this book to all those employers who—knowing full well the enduring tension between capital and labor—nonetheless are willing to craft employment solutions that benefit both workers and managers. Within this forever-tight labor market, building an employee-centered company is no longer a competitive advantage; it is now a competitive necessity.

Contents

A Note from Eastern Bank Foundation

I have been a human resource professional for forty-plus years, working closely with my colleagues to build Eastern Bank into the two-thousand-plus-person organization it is today. I also led the bank's philanthropy efforts for more than twenty years.

For over two hundred years as a community-centered bank, Eastern Bank has been deeply committed to the communities that helped it grow, including doing our part as an employer, advocating for and partnering with others to ensure that the region's workforce is inclusive and reflects the communities we serve every day. Eastern has a corporate culture steeped in social responsibility, economic inclusion, and social justice. So when Jerry and Steve first told me about their book, which brings together the ideas of business success, inclusive workplaces, and shared prosperity, I was immediately on board.

For far too long, too many Americans have been bystanders as economic opportunities have been afforded to some members of our communities and not others. There are real barriers to employment: insufficient education, limited English proficiency, little job experience, and family and social challenges, to name a few. But these barriers can be addressed and removed and should not limit anyone's success. Americans who can and want to work more than they are, or hope to advance to better jobs, are stuck not because these challenges are insurmountable, but because old paradigms drive our thinking and prevent private, public, and nonprofit employers from tapping into deeper talent pools. We should be able to fix this.

For many decades, much of the human resource narrative across corporate America has been dominated by the idea that talent is largely a cost to be minimized. Although this approach may work in very loose labor markets—at least for the employers—it is problematic in times of tighter labor markets. Jerry and Steve make a compelling case that demographic and social trends portend a long period of structurally tight labor markets, and that such an environment requires that many employers rethink how they manage their talent if they want to remain competitive.

Theirs is not simply an economic or political analysis. They provide practical advice and well-documented practices from dozens of employers, large and small, across many industries, who have taken an approach to talent management that is very different from the dominant corporate paradigm. In doing so, exemplary employers are capitalizing on enormous opportunities for their businesses, their employees, and their communities.

Eastern Bank and the Eastern Bank Foundation are leaders on many key policy issues that affect the workforce, including early childhood education, affordable housing, small business development, and workforce training. In 2023, Eastern Bank helped found the MassSkills Coalition—in partnership with Business Roundtable, the Commonwealth of Massachusetts, and the Massachusetts AFL-CIO—to build a community of employers committed to “skills-first” talent management practices that expand who is hired and how employers hire, retain, and advance their workforces. Many of the principles that inspire the coalition and its members are reflected in this volume.

This is the fourth book we have supported. Each one is different, but all seek to advance a timely narrative and focus on building shared prosperity and economic opportunity throughout the communities we serve. I know that we at Eastern Bank will find much to emulate among the many stories and ideas included in this important book. I think you will too.

Nancy Huntington Stager

President and Chief Executive Officer, Emeritus, Eastern Bank Foundation

Introduction

Sailors know well the difference between the shifting winds above, and the hidden, steady current below. Over the past ten years, the US labor market has been buffeted much the same, with labor *demand* shifting dramatically while, hidden beneath the surface, the US labor *supply*—those who are available and willing to work—has slowly, inevitably tightened.

We have written this book to help you, the employer, take practical steps to address the profound impact that a shrinking US labor supply will have on your ability to recruit and retain a competitive workforce.

Over the past ten years, US labor demand has ebbed and flowed: from 2016 through 2020, the US unemployment rate hovered at a "full-employment" rate near 4 percent, then spiked above 14 percent in the midst of the COVID-19 pandemic, only to return within two years to just over 4 percent.[1] By the end of 2025, the rapid introduction of artificial intelligence (AI) technology, combined with the traumatic economic policies of the second Trump administration, injected significant instability in the demand for workers—loosening the labor market for some occupations, such as computer coding, while tightening it for others, such as long-term care.

Yet during this same ten-year period, hidden beneath the turmoil in labor demand, the supply of labor in the US workforce continued to experience a slow, steady constriction that continues to this day: Relatively fewer native-born workers are entering the workforce; a greater percentage are choosing not to work; and an aging baby boom generation is inevitably exiting the workforce.

More abruptly, this systemic tightening of the US labor market has been further exacerbated by the second Trump administration's decision to significantly constrain immigration. Such a dramatic constraint on immigration is of particular importance because, since the beginning of this decade, the US workforce has expanded *primarily* due to the addition of foreign-born workers. You read that right: Since 2020—for demographic reasons we explain later—the number of native-born Americans entering the US labor market had expanded less than 2 percent by the fall of 2025, compared to an increase of nearly 14 percent of foreign-born workers. *Without immigration during this decade, our US labor force would have barely expanded at all.*[2]

* * *

Welcome to our country's emerging "forever-tight" labor market. What will this require of you, the employer? Since the underlying cause of this relentless tightening of labor supply is structural, it is likely that your own organization—whether for-profit, nonprofit, or governmental—will in turn be forced to undertake comparable structural changes in how you find, hire, and retain your workers. Indeed, your workforce strategy may now become as important as your customer-service strategy.

Which is precisely why we wrote this book: to offer you a range of *practical tools* that will help you compete for talent within a forever-tight labor market. Pursuing an employee-focused workforce strategy is no longer merely a competitive advantage; it is fast becoming a competitive necessity.

Einstein Was Wrong

Einstein allegedly claimed, "Insanity is doing the same thing over and over again and expecting different results."[3] Yet Einstein's quote is wrong—or, at most, only half-right. It is correct only if the environment remains static. However, if the environment changes fundamentally, then the opposite is true: Insanity is doing the same thing over and over again and expecting the *same* result.

As the US economy shifts structurally into a forever-tight labor market, employers who continue to deploy the same outdated recruitment and retention workforce strategies over and over again will inevitably discover that they can no longer attract and retain a productive, profitable workforce.

To Our Readers

We offer this book to everyone who has the responsibility for hiring and keeping good staff. Throughout these pages, we speak directly to those of you who are in the business community—owners, managers, workers, investors—constantly struggling to find and keep enough competent staff to meet customer demand. However, we also believe both our analysis and our recommendations are equally valid for those who hire employees within nonprofit and governmental organizations.

In particular, we write to those of you who are among our country's emerging generation of diverse new organizational leaders. You are likely already an owner or manager, or intend to be one soon, responsible for finding and keeping strong, productive workers. In the coming years, you are among those who will shape the future of the US economy—and therefore the broader US culture. It is you we most hope to help thrive within our country's forever-tight labor market.

And Who Might We Be?

Each of us has contributed more than thirty-five years to leading organizations that help employers across the US find, hire, and retain qualified workers. In doing so, our organizations in turn have helped thousands of workers prepare for and secure quality jobs.

Our goal has always been to find common ground between employers and workers, appealing to the shared self-interests of both. We decided to write this book now because experience has taught us that the tighter the labor market, the greater those shared interests.

Still, we are not naïve about how challenging it is for you to find, hire, and retain workers. We assure you that you'll not find us here hawking "ten easy steps to solve your labor needs." Indeed, this is not a two-hundred-page brochure for our consulting services—we both retired from leading our organizations a few years ago—and so we are not attempting to sell you any one proprietary "solution."

Instead, we want to introduce you to a broad variety of well-researched workforce strategies, resources, and potential partners. We suggest you think of this book as a kind of map, one that offers a wide range of recruitment, hiring, training, organizational redesign, and government relations solutions. *You* get to decide where you want to start, and where you hope to arrive. Most importantly, you get to choose your own path.

Book Structure

Chapter 1: The Forever-Tight Labor Market

First, we must convince you that a tight labor supply is here to stay. In their famous *change equation*, strategists Richard Beckhard and Reuben T. Harris emphasized that organizations do not undertake fundamental change until dissatisfaction with the status quo becomes intolerable.[4] Regrettably, we're here to tell you that competing for talent will soon be—if it is not already—your greatest managerial point of pain.

In chapter 1, we underscore that the US labor market is indeed a *market*—with forces on both the demand and supply sides of the equation. Unfortunately, the business media (and even most economists) focus on the demand side, analyzing how the labor market tightens and loosens in response to business cycles and events; that is, they want us to pay attention to the economic *weather*.

Yet equally powerful is the supply side—that is, how many individuals are available and willing to participate in the labor market. That supply of workers also fluctuates, but usually, with the exception of the recent dramatic changes in US immigration policy, much more slowly. It is inexorably determined by deep, structural demographics—particularly the size and age of the US population—as well as by cultural changes in work/life choices. And it is those combined supply-side forces that are now shifting across the US economy, forecasting a profound and lasting change in our economic *climate*.

This first chapter will document those supply-side dynamics. While doing so, we will directly address the implications of US immigration policies as well as demand-side "disruptions," such as AI. In sum, we will document compelling evidence that our US labor supply climate is likely in for a very, very long dry spell.

And that will be it: just one chapter of what psychologists would call *admiring the problem*. The entire remainder of the book is all about practical solutions—what you as an employer can do to find and keep talent within your own organization. In the chapters that follow, we offer three pragmatic, integrated responses to help you compete within the forever-tight labor market:

- *Change how and whom you hire*—by building deep, long-term recruitment relationships across a wider array of both traditional and nontraditional candidate pools.
- *Focus on retention*—by redesigning your jobs and, in doing so, improving efficiency and productivity, which in turn will help you compete for an increasingly diverse *customer* base.
- *Rethink government relations*—by joining with other employers to address employment barriers that constantly impede your finding and keeping good workers.

Combined, these three responses will help you elevate your workforce strategy to the same level of importance as your customer strategy.

Chapter 2: Change How and Whom You Hire

Expansion of the native-born US population is indeed slowing: Workforce participation rates are historically low, and millions of current workers are inexorably aging out. Still, there remain many populations "standing on the sidelines"—people living with disabilities, recent immigrants, people of color and women historically excluded from certain occupations—all willing and able to work, yet still too often outside the reach of conventional recruitment systems.

This chapter describes how to redesign outmoded recruitment practices—such as overly restrictive online applications and applicant-tracking systems as well as unnecessary educational requirements—that screen out potential candidates rather than screening them in. Most importantly, we describe how to partner with organizations that are skilled in finding, training, and supporting pools of candidates who are too often overlooked by conventional recruiters. We also dramatize several brief case studies of businesses that have profited well by "tapping the untapped workforce."

Chapter 3: Focus on Retention

Keep the workers you've fought so hard to recruit. As the labor market tightens, competition for workers between organizations will intensify. Retaining your workforce within that increasingly competitive environment will inevitably require designing a more employee-centric structure and culture.

The hard news: Forging an employee-centered workplace takes creativity, openness, ceaseless effort—and managerial expertise that your organization may well lack. The required degree of change is simply not easy, and to harvest the rewards takes time.

The good news is that a long and deep history of job redesign strategies exists, implemented successfully by employers across diverse industries. This chapter will introduce you to those redesign strategies, as well as to four of the country's most respected job redesign strategists. We also offer several case studies of businesses that have achieved exceptional results—in terms of not only sustained workforce retention but also increased efficiency, productivity, and profitability.

Chapter 4: Rethink Government Relations

In response to the current nationwide labor crunch, many state and national business associations—ranging from health care to manufacturing—now place "access to workers" at the very top of their legislative agendas. Yet in many communities across our country, employers cannot find workers simply because workers cannot find affordable housing; they cannot find childcare or eldercare; they cannot access affordable transportation to work; they cannot afford mental health and long-term health care; and they cannot acquire relevant job training.

The traditional response of many business leaders has long been, "These are social issues, and social issues are not our responsibility." Perhaps, but in a forever-tight labor market, those social issues are fast becoming the business community's biggest challenges. Decades of ignoring these challenges have resulted, inevitably, in a structural underinvestment in the very services that are essential for facilitating the availability of a robust workforce. Given the structural tightening in the US labor market, it is time to rethink the business community's government relations workforce strategy.

In this chapter, we will highlight exemplary business leaders who are now directly challenging this disconnect. Without entangling you in the weeds of policy minutiae, we describe several *business-led* policy and legislative initiatives that have already proven beneficial to employers, workers, and their communities.

Chapter 5: Face Resistance to Change

To restate the obvious: Restructuring your hiring, retention, and government relations strategies will not be easy. The prior chapters will have addressed the most glaring challenges—for example, outmoded recruitment algorithms, lack of job redesign expertise, and inattention to effective public policy solutions.

In this chapter, we dig deeper to address the more obscure challenges that lie beneath: resistance to change within your industry, and likely within your own organization. This resistance includes such hidden elements as structural incentives and disincentives buried deep within your operating systems, possible antiworker biases and other prejudices among management staff, and peer pressure from both your coworkers and fellow business leaders. We will again offer you case histories and examples of business leaders who have exhibited the foresight, and courage, to confront such resistance head-on.

Chapter 6: You Are Not Alone

Finally, the *very* good news, as we underscore throughout this book, is that a diverse range of experienced organizations and partners has traveled this road before you. Some offer their services at a cost; others are free. We have direct experience with many and financial interest in none.

In addition to introducing you to several of the best national resources, we will also assess various types of regional workforce partnerships—from community colleges to management consulting firms, and from nonprofit/public workforce intermediaries to union-affiliated training organizations. The challenge here is that the quality of any particular partnering workforce organization can vary widely. In response, we provide you with guidance on what to ask, and what to look for, when assessing any potential workforce partner's value.

Three Key Themes

Before we dive in, we want to underscore briefly three themes woven for you throughout the book.

Relationships Are Key

First, elevating your workforce strategy so that it is at least equal to that of your customer strategy reveals an essential truth: that both customers and workers are people, not abstractions. Therefore, you will find that *relationships between people* form the core logic threading throughout these pages. Businesses are not numbers; they are organizations alive with thinking, feeling, and creative human beings. All workforce solutions start here.

One Small Step at a Time

Second, in this book, we do *not* suggest that you immediately design and implement all at once a multifaceted, comprehensive plan to address all aspects of your workforce strategy. Instead, it bears repeating that what we have provided for you here is a kind of map—and it is entirely up to you where you want to start, where you are headed, and how quickly you want to proceed. Throughout the book, we urge you to "start small and test widely," for we know from our own experience that, in this ceaseless competition for talent, there is no one correct approach or single best model.

The One Essential "Must"

Third, in keeping with our intent to make this book a type of map, we tried very hard to remove as many "you should . . ." prescriptions as possible. As it turns out, that's easier said than done, though we believe we've done a decent job throughout in offering you a wide range of menus, and relatively few mandates.

However, we do propose one essential *must*: *You **must** talk with your employees*. Talk with your current employees, your prospective employees, even your past employees. And don't just talk, but also listen. Not just once, but always. This is the definition of true leadership. There is simply no other way for you, as a leader in your organization, to build a competitive workforce.

Making It Real

Finally, to help make these workforce solutions come alive throughout the book, we will introduce you to a diverse range of leaders from whom we learned many of our suggested strategies. We hope these brief case studies will highlight that even though competing within a forever-tight labor market will always be a challenge, it can also prove to be an incredibly exciting, creative—and profitable—journey.

Ahead is the first of these case studies. Optimax of Ontario, New York is an exceptionally creative company—and if we were younger men, we would be very tempted to knock on their door and ask for a job.

CASE STUDY: Optimax—the Business Logic of Creativity[5]

Optimax,[6] based in Ontario, New York, designs and manufactures precision optical lenses. Not the kind you balance on your nose, but rather the kind used in the camera system on the Mars rovers; the kind used in the New Horizons spacecraft that took amazing pictures of Pluto; the kind used in quantum computers that direct photons to process information at light speed.

"We make the invisible visible," states Ale' Mendoza, Optimax's director of human resources, "and we mean that in two very different, but parallel ways: First, for our customers, by bending light to reveal the unseen; and second, for our employees, by making the financial and business inner workings of our company transparent."

To craft their highly specialized lenses, Optimax likes to hire widely—from high school grads to PhDs—with particular interest in musicians, gamers, and artists. Those tend to be the types of individuals who are attracted to work as a *craft*, rather than just a job. Optimax does not only train these "nontraditional" employees in the basics of computer numerical control (CNC) technology. From there, the company also launches them on a path of continuous learning—for example, by partnering with the local Monroe Community College and Finger Lakes Community College for customized on-the-job training.

And Optimax is not a small, boutique company with a handful of employees—though it started out that way over thirty years ago, hunkered down in what used to be an old barn on the outskirts of Rochester, New York. Today, Optimax employs more than 450 staff and is recognized as a leader among the more than one hundred other optics-related businesses in the greater Rochester area. In fact, Optimax today is the largest precision optics manufacturer in the United States, with an average revenue growth of 20 percent per year.

Constant Evolution

Optimax is constantly evolving—for evolve it must, as the company continually navigates an optics industry that is experiencing truly existential change. Driving this disruption is a global shift in how information is transmitted and stored: less via electrons and more via photons. The result is revolutionizing semiconductor hardware requirements across the information sector, with Optimax's optical technologies playing a pivotal role in that revolution.

Instead of shrinking its workforce during the COVID-19 pandemic, Optimax experienced the greatest *expansion* in its history in terms of sales, shipments, and hiring. Let's look at a few of the innovations that continue to make Optimax so creatively successful.

Tapping the Untapped, "Nontraditional" Workforce

To get young people excited about optical phenomena, Optimax builds recruitment pipelines all the way down into local elementary schools and works closely with area high schools to establish curricula that embrace emerging optical technologies. These efforts include an educator internship program to expose existing tech-based teachers to real-world experience in the optics industry and to better communicate the value of precision optics employment to students.

Also, Optimax staff regularly present in high school classrooms, meeting directly with students, and their parents, to encourage interning and job shadowing within the company. And, as you'll see later (see Optimax and Community Colleges case study, chapter 6), Optimax has developed a "virtuous cycle" of engagement with local community colleges and vocational technical schools to develop a sustainable pipeline of workers.

Job Redesign

Optimax enables a culture of employee empowerment—using a "power with" versus a "power over" approach—that sets the framework to manage Optimax's more than thirty flexible lean-manufacturing work-cell teams. This allows all employees to own from end to end the entire production of each component. The company also offers a range of nontraditional benefits, including an interest-free loan of up to $2,000 to meet any short-term financial emergency.

Rethinking Government Relations

Led by former CEO Rick Plympton, Optimax worked closely with the US Department of Commerce and the Baldrige Performance Excellence Program to help author the department's national *Job Quality Toolkit.*[7] Optimax continues to embrace the core elements of this toolkit to reinforce best employment practices and remain progressive in attracting and retaining its own competitive workforce. More broadly, Optimax regularly communicates the benefits of the toolkit, raising the bar of employment practices throughout the Rochester region's optics sector.

Forging a Workforce for the Future

As Optimax continues to expand dramatically, Mendoza described two fundamental organizational changes for which he, as HR director, is now responsible when preparing Optimax's workforce of the future:

> Traditionally, Optimax has worked with customers only in the initial phase of product design. Having manufactured the prototype, that was the last we saw of the product. Now, many customers want us to become the prime *suppliers* of those new optical products. And that means co-designing with our customers entirely new systems of manufacturing, which requires a greatly expanded manufacturing workforce having a broad, new range of skills. The impact on our company's culture will be enormous.
>
> Long range, as our founding leaders entered the later stages of their careers, we had to rethink the company's ownership structure. So, we've now embarked on an ownership/governance restructuring called a "Perpetual Purpose Trust" that has three unshakeable bylaws: (1) never sell the company to an outside owner; (2) share at least 25 percent of profits with employees, and (3) ensure that the company stays true to the founders' original purpose of creating value for our customers and financial security for our employees.

That last point means that Optimax will forever advance its leadership as a technological innovator and, in doing so, continue to create ever more and better jobs within its community.

1 The Forever-Tight Labor Market

Now Hiring signs still hang in many storefront windows. Depending on your industry, you've likely posted countless online job openings yourself. Still, it's understandable that you might hold out hope that one day soon the overall US labor market will slacken, and job seekers will once again line up at your doorstep. It's possible, yes—but is it likely?

In fact, the US labor market has been relatively tight for nearly a decade. The only force powerful enough to interrupt a continuous US unemployment rate well below 5.0 percent through 2025 was a catastrophic, global, COVID-19 meltdown (figure 1.1).

And ever since our rapid recovery from the pandemic through the fall of 2025, *nothing* was able to kick the unemployment rate back above *4.3* percent—not the US Federal Reserve's tight money policy, not historically high immigration rates, not erratic tariff policies, not even the heralded onslaught of robots pulsing with artificial intelligence.

Compare that to the prior ten-year period, 2005 through 2015, when the US unemployment rate averaged 7.0 percent.[1] For decades, we in the US employer world had grown accustomed to the assumption of an *over*supply of labor. That oversupply was fueled by the postwar baby boom generation flooding the job market, along with a dramatic increase in the percentage of women leaving home to participate in the world of work. Employers could afford to be picky—even to the point of deploying recruitment systems designed to screen *out* a constant crush of applicants.

When the labor market did occasionally tighten, we were taught to presume that the cause was a nearly rhythmic "business cycle": If currently tight, the labor market would soon again loosen—no need to worry. That perception was encouraged in large part by both the business media and even most mainstream economists, who together constantly focused our

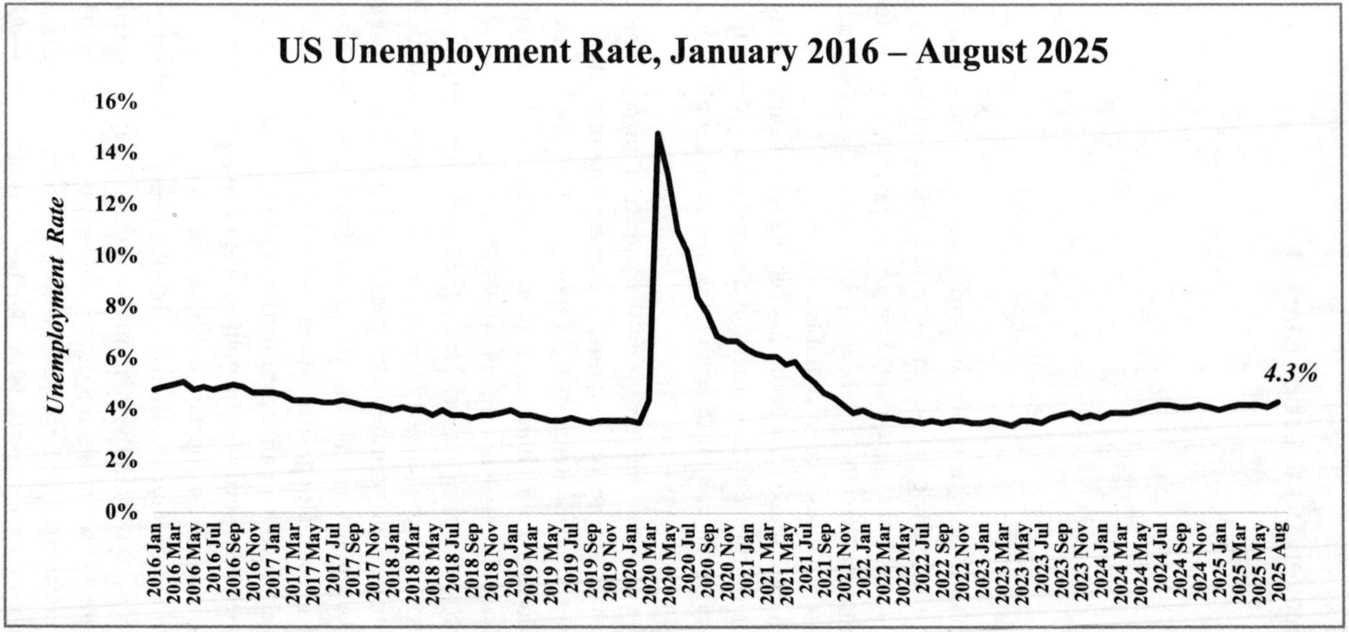

Figure 1.1
US civilian unemployment rate, seasonally adjusted, January 2016–August 2025. *Source:* “BLS Data Viewer,” US Bureau of Labor Statistics, accessed September 29, 2025, https://data.bls.gov/dataViewer/view/timeseries/LNS14000000;jsessionid=DF8B3A019602ED8123705CA1C1936DD9.

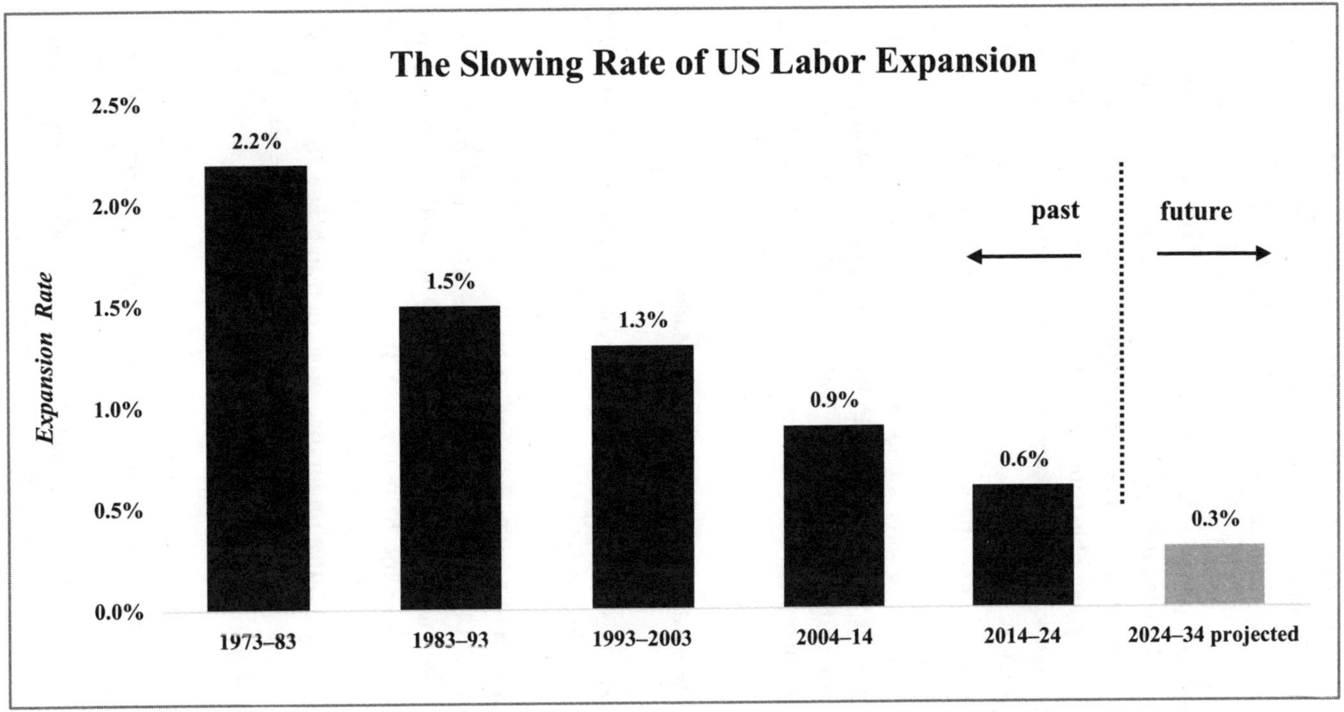

Figure 1.2
US labor force expansion: ten-year compound average annual rates, 1973–2024; projected through 2034. *Source:* Kevin S. Dubina, "Labor Force and Macroeconomic Projections Overview and Highlights, 2023–33," US Bureau of Labor Statistics, *Monthly Labor Review*, August 2024, https://doi.org/10.21916/mlr.2024.14; and "Labor Supply and Factors Affecting Productivity," US Bureau of Labor Statistics, August 28, 2025, https://www.bls.gov/emp/tables/labor-supply-factors-affecting-productivity.htm.

attention on the *demand* side of the labor market—analyzing how labor tightens and loosens in response to business cycles. Essentially, we in the employer community have all been taught to closely watch today's economic *weather*.

However, another powerful force is also at play, for the labor market is indeed a *market*, impacted not just by demand, but also by *supply*. Unfortunately, by ignoring the supply side of the market equation, we have failed to recognize that the rate of expansion in the US supply of labor has been constricting for decades—and is projected to constrict further, well into the 2030s (figure 1.2).

To understand our labor market in full context, we must learn instead how to pay attention to our long-term economic *climate*—for it now appears likely that the US labor supply is headed for quite a long dry spell. And we are not alone in that forecast: In its 2024 report, *The Rising Storm*, the workforce consulting firm Lightcast, which specializes in US labor market analytics, warned that "the U.S. faces a shortfall of millions of workers in the decade to come."[2]

The Profound Restructuring of Our US Labor Market

Why is labor expansion inevitably constricting? The answer can be seen in two simple charts (figures 1.3 and 1.4).

The Slowing Growth of Total Population

Although the total US population continues to expand, the *rate* of that expansion has declined significantly since the 1970s and is projected to decline even further into the 2030s (figure 1.3).

In fact, contrary to the *over*population we were once constantly taught to fear, the US Census Bureau midrange projection indicates that the US population will stop growing entirely by 2080 and—for the first time in the history of our country—will begin to shrink through the end of this century.[3]

The primary cause of our slowing population expansion is simple: Women and men in the US are marrying later in life, are bearing children later in their marriages, and, when they do, are raising fewer children. The required US total fertility birth "replacement rate"—the number of children women must bear to maintain our current population level—is 2.1 babies

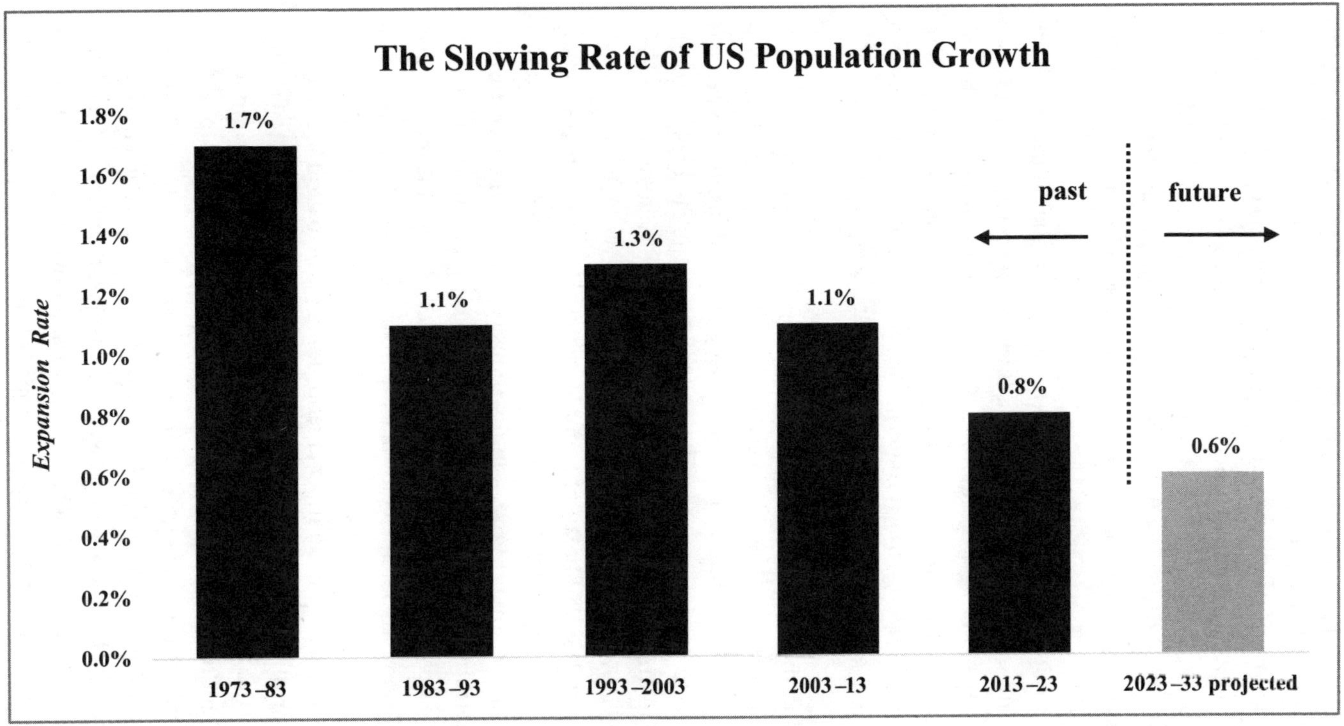

Figure 1.3

US labor population growth: ten-year compound average annual rates, 1973–2023; projected to 2033. *Source:* Kevin S. Dubina, "Labor Force and Macroeconomic Projections Overview and Highlights, 2023–33," US Bureau of Labor Statistics, *Monthly Labor Review*, August 2024, https://doi.org/10.21916/mlr.2024.14.

per woman. Yet during this decade, women in the US are bearing on average fewer than 1.7 babies, the lowest in our country's history.[4]

This slowing birth rate is not simply a US challenge. Except on the continent of Africa, population expansion rates across the globe are also falling: According to the United Nations, the world's total population will *peak* as early as the 2080s.[5] China's population, now 1.4 billion, has already begun to decline and is projected to fall below eight hundred million by the end of the century.

Looking ahead, there's not much we can do about the falling birth rate in the US. And even if we could, from a business perspective—unless you are selling baby clothes—it is irrelevant: A child born today won't enter the labor market until the late 2030s, far beyond your own employment strategy's planning horizon. Unfortunately, the shrinking of our native-born population is already baked into the US labor supply equation.

The Decline in the US Labor Participation Rate

At the same time that our overall *population* growth has slowed, the *participation* rate of the US workforce has also sharply declined, from 66.8 percent in 2001 down to 62.6 percent in August 2025. Of greater concern, that rate is projected to drop still further, down to 61.1 percent, by 2034—the lowest rate since the 1970s (figure 1.4).

According to the US Bureau of Labor Statistics (BLS), male participation in the workforce has dropped dramatically, from 76.3 percent in 2007 down to 70.4 percent in August 2025—and is projected to decline even further to 65.8 percent by 2034. Although the participation rate of women nearly returned to prepandemic levels, it has nonetheless dropped from 60.3 percent in 2007 down to 58.4 percent in September 2025—and is projected to decline further to 56.7 percent by 2034.[6]

The causes of this decline in total labor force participation are many—including the opioid epidemic, an increasing mortality rate due to "deaths of despair," and the fact that the US imprisons the highest number of working-age individuals of any country in the globe.

Yet the greatest cause of our lowering participation rate by far is irrevocably demographic, due to the still-lingering baby boom generation. Even though most baby boomers have now moved past working age, a final baby boom cohort still remains below the age of sixty-five, and therefore the baby boom generation will still account for a considerable portion of the US

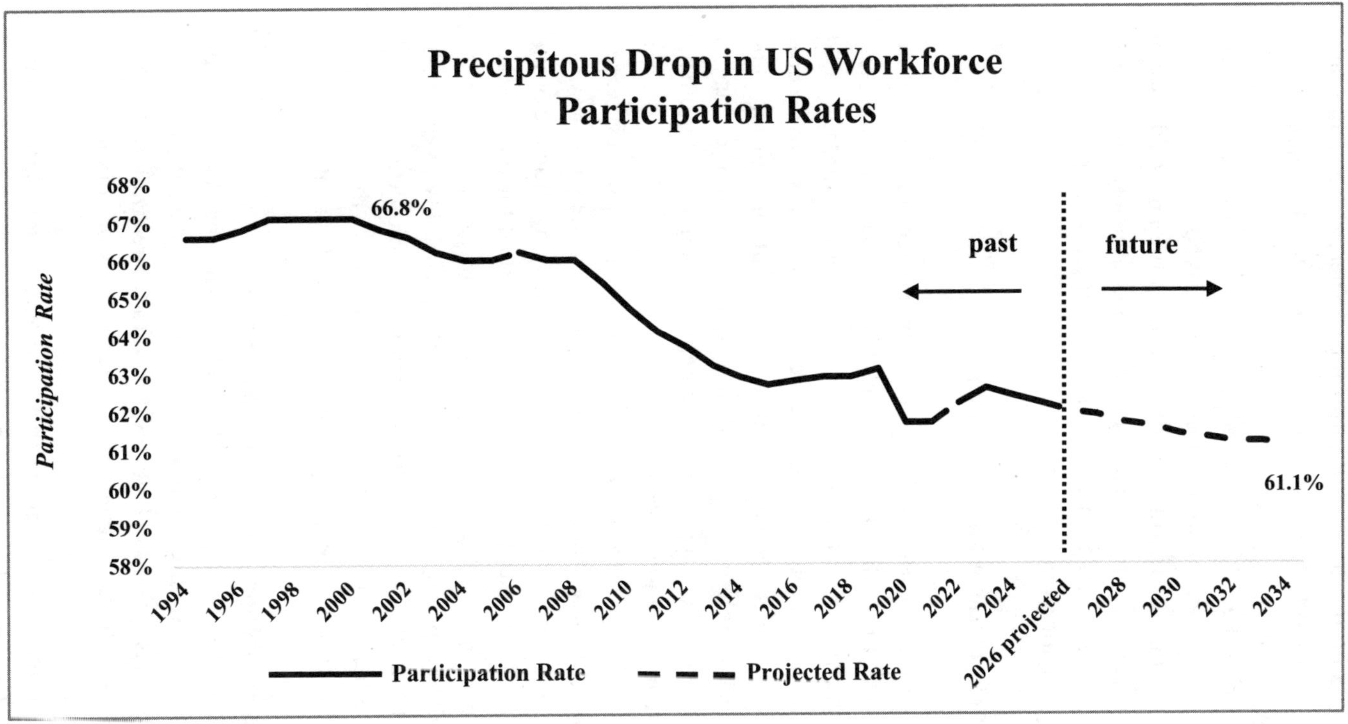

Figure 1.4
US civilian workforce participation rates, 1994 to mid-2025, projected to 2034. *Source:* Kevin S. Dubina, "Labor Force and Macroeconomic Projections Overview and Highlights, 2023–33," US Bureau of Labor Statistics, *Monthly Labor Review*, August 2024, https://doi.org/10.21916/mlr.2024.14; and "Civilian Labor Force Participation Rate by Age, Sex, Race, and Ethnicity," US Bureau of Labor Statistics, accessed August 28, 2025, https://www.bls.gov/emp/tables/civilian-labor-force-participation-rate.htm.

labor force well into the 2030s. Not surprisingly, older workers retire early (leave the workforce *before* the age of sixty-five) at a much faster rate than do younger workers.

In sum, even though the math is not easily self-evident, the relatively high number of *early retirees* from among the *outsized cohort* of baby boomers over the coming decade will account for most of the projected drop in US labor participation. Unfortunately, our disproportionately aging workforce will continue to drive an irrevocable, structural decline in the US workforce participation rate.

Is a Forever-Tight US Labor Market Inevitable?

In a word, no. Certainly, the COVID-19 pandemic taught us that. Within a matter of weeks, the entire global economy nearly ground to a halt, and US unemployment shot well above 14 percent. More recently, the rapid introduction of AI has quickly loosened labor markets for some occupations, such as computer coding and office administration, and for some populations such as recent college graduates, while the abrupt change in US immigration policy has significantly tightened labor markets for others, such as long-term care and construction.

Yet our caution here is *probability*, not prediction. As a business leader, you must make bets based on the best information available. What we are underscoring here is how a seismic shift in the underlying structure of the *supply side* of our labor market has fundamentally slanted the odds toward the future likelihood of a consistently tight labor market.

Still, to address any lingering doubts about the probability of a broader, forever-tight labor market, it is wise to explore in more detail ahead if there are any other factors powerful enough to counteract these structural dynamics—whether on the supply or demand side of the equation.

The Most Important Supply-Side Factor: Immigration

On April 3, 2024, *The Wall Street Journal* ran a story with the headline, "The Jobs Numbers Aren't Adding Up. Immigration Helps Explain Why."[7] With that, the US business press suddenly awakened to the realization that the economy was consistently outperforming expectations not despite immigration, but because of it.

During the three years preceding that *Wall Street Journal* article, both authorized and unauthorized immigration had risen dramatically—the

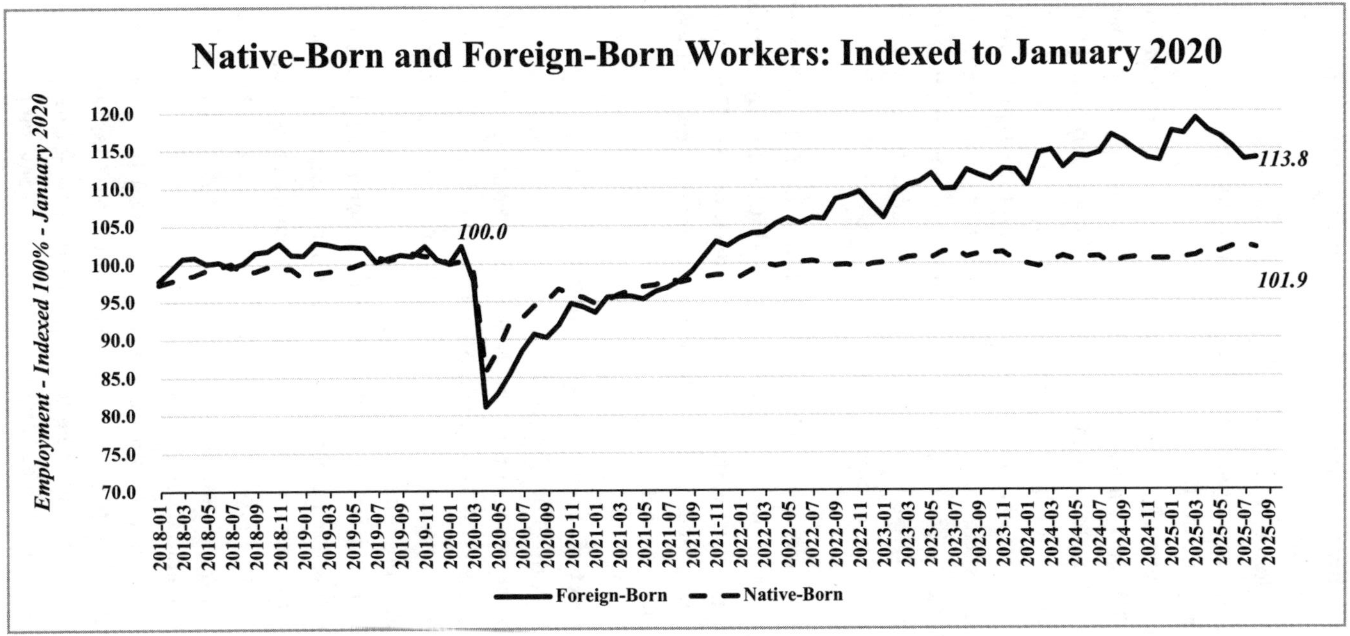

Figure 1.5
US employment levels. Data indexed to 100 percent employment levels at January 2020; not seasonally adjusted. *Source:* Maggie Isaacson and Hannah Rubinton, "Native and Immigrant Employment During the Pandemic," Federal Reserve Bank of St. Louis, *FRED Blog*, December 15, 2022, https://fredblog.stlouisfed.org/2022/12/native-and-immigrant-employment-during-the-pandemic/?utm_source=series_page&utm_medium=related_content&utm_term=related_resources&utm_campaign=fredblog.

largest surge in US history[8]—further inflaming already heated political controversy. Lost amid the resulting media clamor was the fact that since the start of the pandemic, were it not for foreign-born workers entering the labor market, the US would have simply been unable to significantly expand the economy (figure 1.5).

That is, the *net number of native-born workers entering the U.S. workforce has remained relatively flat since early 2020.*[9] For the past five years, the primary reason we have been able to expand the supply side of our labor market has been the net addition of foreign-born workers.[10]

Finally, the importance of immigrants to the US workforce is much more significant than their sheer numbers suggest: Non-native workers who are sixteen or older have a labor participation rate of 68 percent, compared to a 62 percent rate for native-born Americans—and the labor force participation rate among recent immigrants, arriving after 2004, is even higher, at 73 percent.[11]

One conclusion is clear for our US economy: If our future labor market is not to tighten further, the US will require a continued introduction of foreign-born workers, whether documented or undocumented. Continued restriction in the foreign-born workforce will only increase the likelihood of a forever-tight labor market.

The Significant Impact of Federal Immigration Policy

And tighten it will. During 2024, the final year of the Biden administration, federal immigration enforcement policies had already returned to the more restrictive levels of the prior Trump administration's first term.[12] Undeniably, the current policy positions of the second Trump administration are now resulting in an even more dramatic decrease in immigration.

As the Trump administration fulfills its campaign promises, there has already been a significant reduction in the various pathways for future *legal* immigration. This includes an end to both the Temporary Protected Status and Humanitarian Parole programs that together over the past two years have welcomed nearly 1.5 million Haitians, Venezuelans, and others to enter the US legally *and* to receive work authorization.

In addition, the current administration has suspended the US Refugee Admissions Program (USRAP), which had previously allowed approximately one hundred thousand refugees to enter the US annually—nearly 80 percent of whom were of working age and work authorized. Several programs designed specifically to attract highly skilled workers are now also under review. For example, while the H-1B visa program, which largely helps technology industries, had yet to be dramatically revised in 2025, such actions were being seriously reconsidered in the early months of the second administration. Also, reducing the more than one million foreign students coming to study in US universities will clearly have a dramatic effect on the availability of high-skilled labor as more than 20 percent of these students stay on to work in the US, typically in STEM fields.

Dramatically reducing future legal immigration will likely be overshadowed by the deportation of *current* documented and undocumented immigrants. Currently, 2.7 million immigrants reside legally in the United States under the Temporary Protected Status, Humanitarian Parole, and Deferred Action for Childhood Arrivals (DACA) programs combined—and approximately 80 percent of those are of working age and work authorized.[13]

Finally, as each of these time-limited immigration programs expires, we can expect that many currently work-authorized individuals will be detained or deported. Clearly, with the Trump administration's stated commitment to find, arrest, and deport three thousand undocumented immigrants *per day*, we can fully expect that a significant number of the approximately eight million undocumented immigrants now living and working in the United States will be deported. In fact, as of this writing, well over one million immigrant workers have already left the US labor force.[14]

Demand-Side Factors

Throughout this decade, the US has continued its leadership role as the world's most robust economic engine. The more economically powerful we remain domestically and worldwide, the greater the likelihood that our economy will continue to generate ever-greater demand-side pressures, tightening our US labor market even more.

However, we cannot dismiss the possibility that a powerful, *negative*, demand-side factor—another worldwide pandemic, a climatological catastrophe, or any other event causing an economy-wide softening of demand—might one day overwhelm supply-side constrictions and thereby loosen the labor market. Indeed, the second Trump administration's 2025 global tariff policies appear to have already shaken demand for several critical occupations, particularly within the agricultural, retail, and solar energy industries.

To say the least, none of those traumatic events is something to hope for—and in any case, at the firm level, they are all far beyond your control. Yet what you *can* control is twofold: competing more effectively for available workers—which is what this book is all about—and exploring how to reduce your relative need for labor.

As to the latter, efforts to reduce or even entirely replace labor are hardly new. They began when mankind first fashioned tools; those efforts later stoked the industrial revolution; and they have continued apace ever since—right up to that electronic scanner in your local hardware store replacing the teenage checkout clerk. However, what remains true, but is often underappreciated, is that efforts to automate, offshore, and in other ways substitute for domestic labor have all continued at full force throughout the last several decades—and yet we *still* are experiencing a relatively tight labor market.

Artificial Intelligence: The Demand-Side X Factor

Of course, should the business community become convinced that a forever-tight labor market is indeed our future, then pressure to substitute for labor will increase even further. And certainly today, AI vies for the top spot in the list of ways to achieve economy-wide labor substitution.

Pick your favorite economic pundit: In an interview with CNN's Anderson Cooper in May 2025, Anthropic CEO Dario Amodei predicted that AI could automate away up to 50 percent of all entry-level white-collar jobs.[15] Others, like Nobel Prize–winning Dr. Daron Acemoglu of the MIT Sloan School of Management, assure us that over the next decade, AI will threaten at most only 5 percent of US jobs.[16] And still others, like Nobel Prize–winning Dr. Geoffrey Hinton, predict that AI will cause an explosion of workforce productivity,[17] leading to an expansion of consumer wealth and thus spurring demand, which will in turn heighten the need for more workers—tightening the labor market even further.

We have already seen enough now in late 2025 to know that the truth lies somewhere between, with some categories of jobs eliminated, others augmented, and others untouched. This is the shifting *jagged technological frontier* of AI about which researchers at the Harvard Business School warned us in 2023[18]—*jagged* because AI is excellent when performing some tasks, and dangerously inaccurate when performing others.

So far, at least, no evidence yet documents that AI will result in a reduction in the *net size* of domestic employment. Nonetheless, AI and other technological innovations do appear powerful enough to change the *shape* of the labor market. The long-term impact of AI will therefore likely mirror that of prior economy-wide innovations, from the steam engine to electrification: not reducing total nationwide employment, yet very likely *disrupting* large swaths of occupations and perhaps even regional economies.

Should such wide-scale disruption occur, it will fall to the US public sector to respond at a governmental, macroeconomic policy level. Meanwhile, at the firm level, the challenge for you as an employer will be to understand how best to *blend* technological innovation into the new economic reality of a forever-tight labor market—changing how you hire, how you train, and how you support your increasingly limited supply of workers within an increasingly complex technological environment. As Christos Makridis of Gallup has written, "AI is most productive when supporting employees, not replacing them."[19]

The Forever-Tight Labor Market: What Are the Odds?

The massive disruption of the COVID-19 pandemic obscured the reality that the expansion of the supply side of our labor market for years had been irrevocably slowing—distracting us from realizing that today's tight labor market in many industries is not just another cyclical change in the economic weather but is instead a fundamental shift in our economic climate.

Still, as we have conceded, it remains possible that demand-side shocks may again cause widespread US labor markets to soften—that perhaps next month, or next year, most US employers will be able to take down their Now Hiring signs.

So the question remains: As a business leader, where do you want to place your bet? If your bet is that our country has indeed now entered a new economic reality of continued labor scarcity—particularly if your organization is already experiencing hiring challenges—then we believe you will find the remainder of this book a pragmatic exploration of the many, many ways you can prepare for the high probability of a forever-tight labor market.

2 Change How and Whom You Hire

It seems clear that to remain competitive in this forever-tight labor market, you must rethink your talent-acquisition strategy. Your personal leadership here is essential, emphasizing throughout your organization that a fundamental reorientation toward how and whom you hire will soon become an existential necessity.

The business media are rife with complaints by your fellow employers, across widely varying industries, that they "just can't find workers" and that it is hurting their ability to serve their customers.[1] However, at the same time, there are literally millions of individuals who are available and want to work yet are not fully employed. Those millions are our "untapped" talent, and they include the foreign-born, older individuals, caregivers, people living with disabilities, young individuals, ex-offenders, and people of color. We will describe each of these—and how you can find and recruit them—in detail later in this chapter.

But first, let's look at how your current hiring methods might be limiting your ability to tap untapped talent—because far too many employers continue to use recruitment methods and technologies that attract large numbers of applications (many of which are autogenerated) but simultaneously screen out qualified candidates instead of screening them in. Screening in candidates requires changing *how* you hire, which of course will eventually result in changing *whom* you hire.

Retooling *How* You Hire

You may well still be receiving plenty of applications, but what is happening to all those applicants? Employer surveys have documented that 88 percent of employers believed their hiring procedures were *inaccurately* screening out qualified, high-skilled candidates, and that number rose to 94 percent when recruiting for middle-skill workers.[2] And despite spending more, investing in new technologies, and piling ever more work onto the desks of hiring managers, typical US hiring practices are currently taking longer to hire fewer people.[3]

Why do so many hiring managers persist in this behavior despite poor results, increased frustration, and negative consequences? Likely, many managers remain unaware of the compelling evidence of a forever-tight labor market; therefore, they may continue to believe that they are just one business cycle away from a recession. They ask themselves, "Why not just wait?"

Yet it is also likely that many hiring managers are simply not familiar with more effective and efficient hiring methods. Ahead, we provide four strategies for rethinking how and whom you hire: changing requirements, changing systems, changing sources, and changing cultures.

Changing Hiring Requirements

Reexamining hiring requirements is currently receiving increased attention because of the "skills-first" or "skills-based" movement. Grads of Life (GOL; see case study, this chapter), a national leader in this movement, explains that "at its core, embracing skills-first practices means recognizing and prioritizing skills—rather than degrees, jobs histories, or job titles—at every stage of the talent journey."[4]

A deepening array of research is now documenting how companies that recruit candidates for their skills, rather than their college degrees, can substantially increase their talent pools, reduce the "time to hire," and increase retention.[5] OneTen, a coalition of more than sixty employers working to unlock career opportunities for talent without four-year degrees, notes 82 percent of hiring managers surveyed report that skills-first hiring results in more motivated candidates, while 79 percent of hiring managers experience a reduction in "mis-hires" as a result of implementing a skills-first approach.[6]

According to SHRM, the global professional association for human resources (HR) practitioners, 95 percent of executives and HR professionals report that employees with nontraditional credentials perform the same or better than individuals with traditional degrees.[7] Noting this research, many major employers, including PepsiCo, American Express, Chevron, and JPMorganChase, have taken up the mantle of skills-first talent management.

In addition, the US-based Business Roundtable (BR) organization has launched its Multiple Pathways Initiative, through which eighty member companies are participating in a multiyear effort to "reform companies' hiring and talent management practices to emphasize the value of skills, rather than just degrees, and to improve equity, diversity and workplace culture."[8]

Skills-first hiring is not limited to private industry. According to the National Governors Association, more than a dozen governors have removed degree requirements from thousands of state job descriptions. Governor Josh Shapiro of Pennsylvania removed degree requirements from 92 percent of all Commonwealth of Pennsylvania positions, opening nearly sixty-five thousand jobs to individuals without college degrees. Similar steps were taken in Utah and Massachusetts, as well as in Ohio, where Governor Mike DeWine directed that his state include a portal on its website through which applicants could more easily illustrate their skills rather than their degrees.[9]

CASE STUDY: Grads of Life—the "Skills-First" Talent Strategy[10]

Grads of Life[11] is a national initiative of Year Up, the well-known national workforce development organization. Begun in 2014 as a PSA campaign in partnership with the Ad Council, GOL helps companies tap untapped talent through a skills-first talent-management approach.

Founders Elyse Rosenblum and Shawn Bohen, both early leaders in the "inclusive employment" movement, recognized that the best way to connect all Americans to economic opportunity is to leverage the power of the private sector. Rosenblum notes in the ten-year-anniversary report, "Our ambition when we founded Grads of Life was to do something that had not been done before: to catalyze an employer-led movement to end the opportunity divide in America."[12]

Their PSA campaign, which was viewed more than one billion times, showcased the potential for young, diverse talent, even though lacking college credentials, to nonetheless offer skills, experience, and a growth mindset to help companies compete within an increasingly diverse economy.

As support grew, so did Grads of Life. In 2017, GOL published *Dismissed by Degrees*, which was the first widely cited research report to uncover the true cost to businesses of "degree inflation"—that is, requiring unnecessary levels of education as a hiring requirement.[13] Throughout the report, Fuller and Raman emphasized the critical role that skills-based talent management plays in attracting and retaining talent in the face of tight labor markets. Importantly, GOL was an early advocate for diversity, equity, and inclusion (DEI) initiatives to further its skills-first goals.

Since 2017, Grads of Life has expanded its thought leadership to become a full-scale business consultancy, offering a set of tools for companies to assess their hiring practices, develop strategies, and implement skills-first talent-management programs. GOL has also partnered with Business Roundtable to develop an "impact measurement framework playbook" that proposes detailed outcome metrics for businesses to measure the effectiveness of their skills-first talent-management practices.

GOL's impact playbook includes two important tools: the first is an "opportunity identifier" that helps companies evaluate their current hiring practices and identify improvements to create greater value, both for their employees and for their bottom line. The second is an "occupation review" tool that can help a company prioritize which job roles it should first review for improved hiring practices. In addition, the occupation review provides guidance on establishing skills-first career pathways, which in turn help employees more rapidly secure family-sustaining wages.

Currently, GOL works across the country with major business associations, government entities, and dozens of major companies, including Apple, General Motors, Merck, and JPMorganChase. According to Aneesh Raman, chief economic opportunity officer at LinkedIn, "Over the last decade, Grads of Life has led from the front in the shift to a skills-first approach to talent. Their efforts have influenced major employers to think differently about human potential and their impact has been felt far and wide by professionals who were previously locked out of opportunity, despite bringing all the right skills and abilities."[14]

Your company's hiring managers may well believe that requiring degrees for their positions is necessary, and in many cases they are correct. Many jobs require specific degrees and/or certifications, often to meet licensure or other legal requirements—yet, importantly, many do not. Alicia Sasser Modestino of Northeastern University and other researchers have documented that degree requirements are more elastic than you might realize, rising in times of loose labor markets and declining in tighter times.[15]

Understandably, even for those positions that do not require a specific educational threshold, a degree may well serve as an easy proxy—yet the result is too often a profound, unnecessary restriction of qualified candidates. According to the Burning Glass Institute, unnecessary degree requirements eliminate nearly two-thirds of otherwise eligible American workers.[16]

Your first step is to assess your own company's current hiring requirements. Easily available assessment tools include Grads of Life's opportunity identifier,[17] as well as Business Roundtable's detailed "skills validation" process published by its Multiple Pathways Initiative.[18]

In completing your hiring requirements analysis, your company will have identified which jobs have large numbers of persistent openings; among those many openings, the low-hanging fruit will be the positions that truly do not require degrees. Also, your company will then be able to rewrite job descriptions that reflect the *actual* skills needed for a position—an illuminating process in itself, usually neglected when relying solely on educational proxies.

While you're at it, your company may want to revisit overly rigid "work experience" and "work continuity" hiring requirements. Certainly, experience matters, but work experience and continuity are not the same as work *skills* and may not accurately predict future successful job performance.

For example, two important segments of untapped talent, caregivers and young workers, are negatively impacted by rigid length and continuity requirements. Many women take time off to care for their young children, only to find that, upon returning to the job market, they are locked out of positions for which they are still highly qualified. Similarly, while attending school, many young workers may hold multiple part-time jobs—through which they are in fact accumulating a significant array of work skills—yet they are then punished in the job market for not having held significant full-time positions.

During your company's assessment of its hiring practices, you might also examine whether some of your job descriptions have "ballooned" over time—with many new requirements piled on top of prior requirements—resulting in a position description that no real-world applicant could ever truly fulfill. Rewriting job descriptions requires a fair bit of work, yet the payoff includes not just broader recruitment pools but also more concise descriptions that will in turn support more effective performance and career advancement opportunities.

Finally, recent evidence reporting on the skills-first movement suggests both good and bad news. The good news is that many companies have taken significant steps to reduce or eliminate unnecessary degree requirements, including in biotechnology (Vertex), manufacturing (General Motors), airlines (Delta), and computers (IBM).[19]

The bad news is that there still remains a significant gap between intent and results. In one recent study, dozens of companies reduced or eliminated degree requirements, yet the share of workers hired without a bachelor's degree within those same companies increased by only 3.5 percent from 2014 to 2023.[20] Several problematic hiring practices contribute to such poor results, including continued reliance on outmoded recruitment and hiring systems, to which we turn next.

Changing Hiring Systems

Whether your company is large or small, it has likely created several systems designed to manage the never-ending challenge of finding and keeping productive workers—not to mention colleagues you like and enjoy working with. Those systems are applied at three phases of the talent acquisition process: recruitment, hiring, and onboarding/support.

Recruitment HR management is increasingly dominated by technology. Most US employers now use software systems, known generically as *applicant-tracking systems* (ATSs), to track job candidates throughout the recruitment and hiring process. When combined with job boards and online applications, the entire hiring cycle is increasingly automated—and now further augmented by AI. More than four thousand software-based tech vendors serve corporate HR departments, and companies of all sizes are consistently increasing their spending on these systems.[21]

Automated hiring technologies arose in the 1990s from the need to manage the growing flood of applications from the internet revolutionizing how and where jobs were posted, allowing applicants to more easily apply for multiple positions, often without any meaningful job-matching criteria or qualifications. An ATS and other linked technologies offer efficient management of enormous numbers of applications.

Ironically, these systems and their algorithms too often automatically screen out highly qualified candidates who are the very untapped talent hidden in plain sight within the available labor force. These systems too often squeeze out the human interactions and relationships that are so effective in recruiting and retaining "good fit" talent at all levels.[22]

As we have noted, hiring often begins with poorly crafted job descriptions, but it is then narrowed further by overreliance on technology. Many applicants are frustrated by online barriers, such as limited internet service and application platforms that are not disability friendly, as well as perhaps by their own limited English competency or limited experience navigating technology. Given all those frustrations, many qualified job seekers may well screen *themselves* out to begin with, not even attempting to start the online process. If applicants do succeed in submitting applications online, then the ATS algorithms can, as we have shown, pose the next barrier, rejecting applicants who cannot meet overly rigid work experience, certification, or degree requirements.

According to SHRM, 45 percent of HR professionals say their organization uses an ATS, but only 32 percent say their ATS recognizes credentials earned through nontraditional pathways. SHRM estimates that more than 50 percent of qualified applicants are unable to make their way past the online ATS screening algorithms.[23]

Fortunately, ATS and related technologies are increasingly sophisticated, which means they can be adjusted to widen rather than narrow the hiring funnel. For example, if intentionally directed to do so, ATS algorithms can now reflect revised job descriptions that focus on skills rather than skill proxies and can more accurately avoid narrow definitions of broad work experience.

In addition, these algorithms can now be more carefully crafted to avoid biased terminology and can be integrated with online job boards that are known for attracting more diverse talent. For example, Applied has created a technology platform that automates the skill-requirements process and allows hiring managers to easily develop task-based skill assessments.[24]

Hiring Despite the dominant use of technology in the recruitment phase, many hiring managers continue to turn to old-fashioned methods to determine their final hiring decisions. In particular, hiring managers over-rely on poorly structured interpersonal interviewing, a reliance that appears to be increasingly inefficient; according to Glassdoor, the time spent by employers to interview candidates has nearly doubled since 2009.[25]

Although in-person interviewing is an important tool, it is worth the effort to reduce as much bias as possible by standardizing questions, designing consistent ranking systems, incorporating skills-first assumptions, and sharing the interview process among as diverse a group of managers as possible. For example, both Ernst & Young and Microsoft have entirely revamped their interview processes to increase their hiring of neurodiverse candidates. Rather than the traditional, unstructured, face-to-face interview, candidates participate in a week-long process that simulates a workday, within which applicants are asked to complete tasks and solve complex problems with other candidates, thereby also testing their team-participation skills.[26]

CASE STUDY: Spaulding Rehabilitation Hospital—the Interactive Interview[27]

Elyse Forbush, former director of nutrition and food services for Spaulding Rehabilitation Hospital,[28] one of the nation's leading rehabilitation hospitals, created a simple and brief *interactive interview* that includes ten minutes of conversation about the candidate's interest and availability, a fifteen-minute walk around the facility to gauge the candidate's listening and learning skills, and twenty minutes of hands-on exercises using actual work materials to gauge their skills and learning ability.

This skills-based interview method, which is paired with a skills-based résumé template provided to applicants prior to submitting their résumé, was originally developed for applicants with disabilities. It is now used for all applicants and has been widely adopted by several other Spaulding departments.

Onboarding and Support Once you fill a position, which is inevitably expensive and time-consuming, the first several months are crucial for determining the fit between the new hire and your company. It is important to acknowledge that, compared to more conventional candidates, new hires from untapped talent pools may face relatively greater onboarding challenges as they adjust their schedules, expectations, and ongoing life challenges to their new jobs. You will benefit by anticipating these challenges via a well-planned, sophisticated onboarding process.

For example, Homebridge, a Bay Area home care provider, learned directly from its employees and developed an integrated recruitment, training, and onboarding process. It includes support for English-language learners and is now the company's standard procedure.

CASE STUDY: Homebridge—Solving the Caregiver Shortage Through Worker-Centered Innovation[29]

"When the pandemic hit, we had to adapt—or risk losing everything."

As COVID-19 swept across the globe, few industries were as deeply impacted as health care and long-term care. For Homebridge,[30] a San Francisco–based nonprofit providing in-home services to complexly diagnosed older adults and people with disabilities, the stakes couldn't have been higher. "Homebridge's clients are some of the most vulnerable people in our city," explained Serena Maria, senior manager of programs. "They didn't just need care, they needed wraparound supports to access that care and follow-up to ensure their needs were met."

As San Francisco scrambled to address this unprecedented economic crisis and rising homelessness, Homebridge became a linchpin in one of the city's boldest initiatives: Project Roomkey. This statewide program aimed to house homeless individuals in hotels, and Homebridge was tasked with providing wraparound home care services for these newly housed residents. "We weren't just caregivers anymore," Rhowana Gandy, former caregiver and current supervisor, shared. "We were a bridge to housing and a soft space to land."

A New Reality for Caregivers

The clients that Homebridge served changed overnight. Many had experienced years of homelessness, untreated health issues, and deep trauma. Caregivers were suddenly navigating not just physical care but also complex behavioral health challenges. "Our caregivers were working in supportive housing buildings in the Tenderloin—a neighborhood hit hard by the pandemic and the opioid crisis," recounted a longtime caregiver, Freddie Gilbert. "It felt like we were on the frontlines of every crisis at once."

Demand for Homebridge's services soared. But the workforce—already strained—began to dwindle. Older caregivers retired early to protect their health. Others left to care for young children or sick family members. Recruitment became a Herculean task, as government aid for those choosing not to work and the health risks of caregiving combined to make the job less attractive. Within the first year of the pandemic, Homebridge lost nearly a third of its workforce. "It was heartbreaking," said Lali Sells, project manager. "The team was giving everything they had, but it often felt like it wasn't enough."

Reimagining Caregiver Support Through BUILDE

Even before the pandemic, Homebridge had been an industry leader in providing union wages, benefits, and robust training in partnership with organizations like the Paraprofessional Healthcare Institute (PHI).[31] Yet the pandemic underscored the need for a more holistic approach—one that centered the voices of caregivers.

This realization led to the creation of the BUILDE Initiative (belonging, unity, inclusion, leadership, diversity, and equity). "The philosophy was simple but radical," explained Meaghan Shanahan, senior director of programs. "Our caregivers are the foundation of everything we do. If they're not thriving, neither are our clients."

The BUILDE Initiative began by bringing caregivers and administrative staff together in focus groups and interviews to identify challenges and cocreate solutions. "It wasn't just about listening," recalls Ben Safer, finance operations analyst. "It was coming together to cocreate solutions."

One innovative aspect of the BUILDE Initiative was that it commissioned a "secret shopper" report: A caregiver not currently employed by Homebridge was contracted to experience Homebridge's recruitment, training, and onboarding processes firsthand. Their findings, presented anonymously at first, led to immediate reforms. "When the secret shopper revealed themselves and met with staff, it was a game-changer," Shantel Weingand, Homebridge CFO, recalled. "Hearing direct feedback in such a personal way made the need for change undeniable."

Key Reforms Spark Transformation

The insights gained from BUILDE drove a series of impactful changes:

- *Community-based recruitment:* Collaborations with local organizations prioritized candidates with the right values and skills over formal experience.
- *Enhanced training:* A hands-on shadowing program paired new caregivers with seasoned staff, creating a supportive learning environment.
- *Redesigned workspaces:* The office was transformed into a welcoming hub for caregivers, fostering connection and belonging.
- *Wage increases:* Substantial raises made caregiving a more viable long-term career.

Launching the Vocational English Program

One of many significant outcomes of BUILDE was the development of the Vocational English as a Second Language (VESL) Program. Many caregivers had shared their desire to improve their English skills while working, seeing it as both a professional and personal growth opportunity. "Caregiving wasn't just a job for them—it was a way to build a future," said Ripa Saha, senior manager of talent development.

With funding from the California Workforce Development Board, Homebridge partnered with health care union SEIU-2015, the San Francisco Office of Economic and Workforce Development, and the Mission Economic Development Association to design the program. Over three months, participants received intensive English instruction tailored to caregiving, paired with on-the-job training.

The impact was profound. "I am very grateful for this opportunity, providing us with excellent training which makes our work as a professional possible and at the same time, allows us to improve our English so that our services are of the highest quality for the clients," shared Cesar Lopez, a graduate of the program. Clients also appreciated the opportunity to support their caregivers' growth: "When a caregiver and client come together, they have to meet each other at a mutual level," said Mystica Talbot, a Homebridge client. "Even with the language barrier, I am able to help my caregiver to practice English, and being able to both help each other, brought us closer together."

Building a Resilient Workforce

The BUILDE Initiative and VESL Program didn't just solve immediate challenges; they also redefined what a worker-centered organization could achieve. Today, Homebridge boasts a more resilient workforce, in which caregivers feel valued, supported, and empowered. "Investing in our caregivers isn't just the right thing to do," said Homebridge's new CEO, Min Chang, "it's the only way forward. No one understands what it takes to deliver exceptional care, day in and day out, more than our frontline staff."

Homebridge's story offers a blueprint for organizations grappling with similar challenges. By centering worker voices, reimagining recruitment and training, and designing inclusive training and employment, Homebridge proves that innovation in job quality isn't just possible: It's transformative.

Effective onboarding can start with training *supervisory* managers, to make them aware of the unique challenges that such nontraditional hires might encounter and to provide those supervisors with practical tools to support their new, nontraditional staff. In addition, identifying and training *peer mentors*—experienced staff whose role is to support, not supervise, new hires—can make a huge difference while those new employees learn the ropes.

You might also consider creating a formal program that offers new employees a chance to check in with and receive support from a formal coach. A *coach* differs from a peer mentor in that the coach is typically a senior staff person whose primary role is to help the employee improve overall competence, acquire particular skills, or achieve a specific goal. A *peer mentor* is literally a peer—someone who holds or has held a position equivalent to the employee's—whose role is to help the new hire integrate into the culture, learn answers to day-to-day questions about job-specific experiences, and in general receive a degree of emotional and psychological support. Both the coach and peer mentor differ from a *supervisor*—no matter how "supportive" that supervisor might be—in that the supervisor still retains performance and disciplinary accountability over the employee.

One coaching resource we recommend is Employer Resource Networks (ERN USA), which has created a model for small to midsize companies to share "success coaches" using a platform that provides case management, program metrics, and reporting capabilities. ERN USA also provides assistance to help companies organize job-retention services, work supports, and training programs for employees.[32]

Do It Yourself: Employer-Embedded Training Finally, if your company is large enough and has the resources, you might consider implementing an employer-embedded mentoring, coaching, and training model. The advantage of this approach is that you can fully design and control every aspect of your hiring process, all within your own company's employee-centered strategy. Cooperative Home Care Associates (CHCA), a 1,750-worker, employee-owned home health care agency headquartered in the Bronx, has for decades deployed that model in cooperation with PHI[33] with documented success.

CASE STUDY: CHCA Training Program—the Business Logic of Relationships[34]

How do you train thousands of unemployed women of color *and* provide them stable jobs? You build a company that embeds training and employment within a single, seamless strategy.

Cooperative Home Care Associates,[35] headquartered in the Bronx and employing 1,750 personal care and home health aides, has honed that strategy for more than thirty-five years. Its "employer-embedded" entry-level training program is wholly designed, managed, and staffed on-site *within* the company—making it distinct from conventional "third-party" training programs that may train low-income individuals for a specific occupation, but rarely for a specific employer.

CHCA's documented success in providing stable employment for thousands of predominantly Latina and African American women is often attributed primarily to its worker-owned structure: With its 1,750 employees, CHCA is the largest democratically structured worker cooperative in the United States. Yet the true secret of CHCA's success in attracting and retaining workers—within an industry infamous for high staff turnover—is its seamless continuum of recruitment, selection, training, employment, and support.

As CHCA's CEO and president, Adria Powell, emphasizes, "I see each day the unique value of training our own staff, rather than relying on third-party trainers. For our aides, the consistency between their training and their day-to-day work creates a deep sense of confidence."

From the job seeker's perspective, CHCA's training model works because it

- *guarantees employment* to every enrollee who successfully graduates from CHCA's embedded training program;
- *minimizes gaps* in the job seeker's journey throughout the often intimidating process of finding an appropriate training program, graduating, being hired, and then maintaining employment; and
- *maximizes the consistency* of expectations throughout those transitions, in terms of knowledge, skills, attitudes, and adherence to company policies—all tailored to CHCA's specific structure and culture.

What this means for the employer is that as the candidate moves through CHCA's seamless, supportive employment system, over time she builds multiple *relationships* with a wide range of CHCA staff. It is this intentional layering of supportive, trusting relationships that lies at the heart of CHCA's success in attracting and retaining its workforce. "From the first day they step into the office," says Powell, "our aides experience a culture of belonging and inclusivity. And as they come to realize that 40 percent of the *administrative* staff themselves started out here at CHCA as home health aides, they understand that this is a company that's built around *them*, as well as their home care clients."

Following a Typical CHCA Job Applicant

To dramatize how CHCA minimizes gaps, maximizes consistency, and builds relationships, follow the path of a typical job applicant, who we'll call Paulina. Paulina is a Latina woman and a single mom of two young children. Although she has little formal employment experience, Paulina nonetheless possesses considerable personal caregiving skills, having cared for her elderly mother in her native Dominican Republic.

The Open House

Seeking work as a personal care and home health aide, dually certified in New York State, Paulina first attends a CHCA open house held at the agency's main office in the Bronx. The open house is conducted by the same staff who lead CHCA's workforce development and training program, and they are quite straight with Paulina: Not everyone graduates from the training program, home care work is complex and can be emotionally challenging, and home care hours are not nine to five.

Still, Paulina likes what she hears—not least of all that CHCA's three-week training program is free. Also, CHCA offers the training program in both English and Spanish—and Paulina knows she will learn more easily if she can study in her native language.

First Days of Training

Paulina enters her classroom located at the same company offices where she knows she will be employed after she graduates. There she learns that her lead trainer is a home care nurse who herself had started as a home care aide at CHCA—and that the assistant trainer as well had worked as a home health aide at CHCA for many years.

Consistent Expectations

Paulina soon realizes she is not simply being trained to become a home care aide: She is being trained to be a *CHCA* home care aide. She must arrive on time, every day; make sure her children have reliable daycare; wear a clinical uniform with no loose jewelry; and, most importantly, she must treat her trainers—and her fellow classmates—with dignity and respect.

By watching how CHCA supports its trainees while holding the line on disciplined expectations, Paulina soon realizes that CHCA isn't just training graduates they will never see again: They are training their own future employees.

Graduation

Paulina was excited when she received her dual personal care and home health aide certificate. She knew exactly with whom she would soon be working: not only with her fellow graduates—several of whom had become her friends—but also her supervising coordinator, who herself had been promoted after working several years as a CHCA aide.

Employment—with Additional Support

And Paulina has additional backup as well, in the form of her assigned peer mentor—again, a former CHCA aide. Paulina can call upon her mentor to share her fears, and even her mistakes, because she knows her mentor is there to guide and support, not judge her performance.

Relationships Are the Key

As this walkthrough dramatizes, compared to a typical third-party training experience, CHCA offers multiple opportunities for prospective employees like Paulina to develop consistent, lasting relationships *within* the organization. Each new relationship binds the CHCA employee closer to the company, both improving care quality and increasing employee retention.

Powell reflects, "To me, there is a grounding effect for the recent graduates, knowing they will continue to work with staff who supported them and guided them in training. They've already built a sense of connection to their coworkers and members of the administrative staff when they ride in the elevators or settle in for a meal in the kitchen areas to have lunch. All of which helps build bonds and connection to the organization, staff, and each other."

Changing Hiring Sources

Ironically, as technology has taken hold of hiring systems, many recruiters are doing workarounds by turning back to the traditional practice of simply "who-you-know" networking.[36] As a result, your recruiters and hiring managers are still likely over-relying on their preexisting professional, educational, and social networks for candidates.

This means that untapped workers—who may be new to the workforce, or even new to the area—will remain at a distinct disadvantage, far outside your colleagues' familiar outreach efforts. Unfortunately, personal referral connections tend to mirror and reinforce predominant hiring imbalances: "People tend to know—and therefore recommend—people like themselves," according to Ruth Thomas, chief of research and insights at Payscale, a compensation management firm.[37] Therefore, consider the following alternative hiring sources.

Informal Hiring Networks To broaden their *sources* of talent, what your recruitment colleagues require is a very structured strategy, reaching far outside their comfort zones and exploring entirely different sources of talent. Those include *informal* social networks and community-based organizations frequented by untapped workers in their everyday lives—for example, churches, sports clubs, and fraternal and sororal groups—a strategy we will focus on in more detail in chapter 6 on partnerships.

Community and Technical Colleges Thinking about more formal settings, an essential source of untapped talent is the community and technical college system, extending throughout nearly every American community. Because these education and training institutions are far less expensive than four-year colleges, they tend to attract relatively more limited-income individuals, new immigrants, and racially diverse students seeking a cost-effective path to workforce success.

In the best of cases, community and technical colleges can be encouraged to partner with employers to develop tailored internships, forging a dedicated talent pipeline that funnels trained applicants directly into the recruitment networks of participating businesses. (See Optimax and Community Colleges case study, chapter 6.) In addition, federally funded One-Stop Career Centers often field job fairs, helping connect employers with nontraditional candidates.

Community Service Organizations Your community likely contains a range of service organizations whose missions specifically include job training, matching, and employment support services for nontraditional workers. Many of these agencies form dedicated recruitment and training partnerships with local businesses. For example, three major health care systems in Massachusetts—Beth Israel Deaconess, Boston Children's Hospital, and Mass General Brigham—have built sophisticated recruitment and screening pipelines in partnership with community-based providers.[38]

Technology-Based Solutions Technology-based solutions offer the most recent innovations to tap untapped talent. For example, more than 400 employers use the Untapped Solutions website to find workers—drawn from pools of formerly incarcerated as well as homeless individuals—for the retail, technology, and manufacturing industries.[39] Other organizations that host online job matching sites for untapped talent include Black Jobs,[40] a job board for African American professionals; and the Mom Project,[41] a job board focusing on working mothers.

Third-Party Recruitment Firms If your company contracts with a third-party recruitment firm, you might consider setting explicit expectations, requiring your contractor to move away from sole reliance on traditional sources of talent. For example, you can require your contractor to build dedicated pipeline relationships with community, government, and other social service organizations. Changing your contractor's recruitment habits won't be easy, but it will certainly occur more quickly if you, their client, require it.

Paid Work-Based Experience and Apprenticeship Programs With or without an external partner, paid "work-based experience" training programs are another excellent way to attract untapped talent. Many untapped workers who are offered the opportunity to be paid while being trained—particularly when coupled with the promise of guaranteed employment upon competition of training—are now being coaxed into the labor market.

The best-known and most widely tested example of work-based experience programs is the apprenticeship (typically, though no longer exclusively, cosponsored by a labor union), which historically has been the primary pipeline method for the construction trades.[42] Now, with the help of increased federal and state government funding, apprenticeships are expanding into many other industries, from childcare to financial services.

There are also other less formal, shorter-term, paid-work-based learning models. For example, Boston Children's Hospital was having great difficulty recruiting animal care technicians, a key position supporting their large research operations. The hospital first determined that they could remove unnecessary, onerous educational requirements for that position, after which they then partnered with a community-based organization to develop an eight- to twelve-week, paid training program that ensures full-time employment upon successful completion. The program, which has been operating for six years, has successfully recruited and retained dozens of new technicians.[43]

Your Own Employees as a Recruitment Gold Mine Finally, one obvious source of talent that is remarkably underutilized is your own workforce. Less than one-third of US corporate vacancies are filled from within organizations—a dramatic change from years past, when internal advancement, accompanied by backfilling, was the norm. As researcher Peter Cappelli has thoroughly documented, talent developed internally often performs better than outside hires, and this approach reduces turnover. Yet despite its documented advantages, development of internal talent continues to decline.[44]

Unfortunately, workers of color, women, and people with disabilities are disproportionately employed in lower-level positions, where they are often "stuck at the bottom." In response, you can design and implement the necessary infrastructure and programming—with a strategic focus on career advancement—to develop your own workers' untapped talent.

In that effort, carefully articulated career ladder programs are key, providing lower-level employees with transparent, meaningful, and realistic pathways to higher-level positions. In addition, peer mentors and coaches can be critically important, ensuring that frontline employees are able to learn what advancement opportunities exist, what resources are available to help them advance, and how to navigate the best advancement pathway. Most importantly, you must ensure that your managers are not only on board with the program but also explicitly *incentivized* to consider and hire qualified internal candidates.

Developing talent *internally*—particularly diverse talent—provides an enormous boost for recruiting untapped talent *externally*. Diverse candidates regularly report that seeing company leadership and recruitment managers "who look like me" is a top reason for accepting a position. Internally referred hires also tend to be high performers, contributing both to increased retention and profitability.[45] With meaningful career advancement programs and increasing numbers of diverse managers in place, you can then look to your own employees as important sources of referrals of untapped talent—and, no small point, you can thereby reduce what you pay to outside recruiters.

Finally, referral bonuses are a well-known tool for encouraging employee referrals and certainly should be in your recruitment toolbox. Yet it is your employees' true enthusiasm and belief in your company as a supportive environment for untapped talent that is the far more powerful tool. If your employees know that they are appreciated, supported, fairly compensated, and have opportunities for advancement—then they will become your best recruiters.

Changing Your Hiring Culture

Reshaping your company culture so that you can successfully recruit untapped talent begins with believing that talent is a necessary competitive investment, rather than simply an expense to be minimized. The disappointing results to date from corporations that proclaim their intent to hire nontraditional employees yet fail to actually hire very many tell us that changing how and whom you hire cannot simply rely on good intentions; instead, it requires changes in behavior—and that requires changes in organizational culture. As Erin White, senior director of Business Roundtable, says, "Rewriting job descriptions is the easy part. The hard work is internal culture change, and changing culture and practices is very hard."[46]

Leadership Changing organizational culture is one of the most challenging tasks for a leader. Although such change must be embedded from top to bottom, to be successful, you *personally* must embrace and champion it. Designing new incentives and training is important, but nothing is more important than thoughtful, consistent, and persistent messaging—and behavior—from the top.

Therefore, when competing in a forever-tight labor market, leaders can emphasize three messages throughout their organization:

- Talent is key to the business's competitive success and therefore worthy of investment.
- Expanding whom you hire to include nontraditional workers is not a "nice to have" but a strategic "must have."
- Untapped talent can indeed be found and developed, but only if the business is willing to make the investments of time and resources necessary to find, recruit, and retain nontraditional workers.

These messages are most effective when repeated consistently, through every available avenue and format. From celebrating successes to reporting on data, changing culture is a never-ending campaign to strengthen the core inner workings of your organization.

Management Training The business literature is replete with stories of CEO-led "culture change" campaigns that fail when they try to operationalize. Tapping untapped talent is no different. Although senior leadership may well pronounce that the organization is changing whom and how it hires, it is always the midlevel hiring managers who actually *do* the hiring, and they will require specific training on both *why* widening the hiring funnel is important and *how* it can be successfully implemented.

To begin, first field an honest assessment of the status quo, detailing both your failures and successes in attracting and retaining untapped talent. In particular, identify the structural and personal biases built into the company's current hiring and retention systems.

This initial analysis should include helping your staff, and yourself, learn more about nontraditional workers: who they are; why they might be likely to work in your particular business; what their lives and communities are like; what the different networks are through which they receive trusted information; and, most importantly, what are both their challenges *and* their assets.

In this analysis, engage as participants any of your current employees who themselves were initially considered untapped talent. They alone can provide the type of direct and honest insights that your hiring managers are unlikely to otherwise possess.

Incentives All the campaign rhetoric and training—however well-intentioned—will fall flat if your current incentives structure remains in place. Hiring managers are judged and financially incentivized largely by the volume of their hires and how quickly they fill those open positions. These incentives make them reluctant to seek out harder-to-reach alternative networks or to hire nontraditional candidates.

In reordering the priority of your company's hiring metrics, performance data that emphasize cost minimization and speed should be supplemented, if not entirely replaced, by data that measure "the magnitude and duration of their value added to the organization."[47] Adding tangible financial incentives within a *hiring* manager's performance review to reward "skills-first" hiring—and, importantly, adding financial incentives to reward skills-first promotions by *supervisory* managers—will have an enormous impact on changing behavior, ultimately strengthening the company's competitive advantage in the labor market.

Data Any skills-based talent management initiative will be made stronger if you perform an initial data-informed analysis of your company's current status and then track progress carefully and transparently over time. You, and all your hiring staff, will want to know how well and how quickly you are hiring and promoting a more diverse and skills-based workforce. And then you will want to correlate that data over time to learn how these new hiring outcomes impact your operational productivity and business profitability.

Once you have this data, you can use it to motivate your colleagues, refine and expand your skills-first initiatives, and promote your company more effectively to potential applicants. As noted earlier, you don't need to reinvent the wheel here; for example, Business Roundtable has partnered with Grads of Life to develop a detailed measurement framework for skills-based talent management initiatives.[48]

CASE STUDY: Messer Construction—the Business Logic of Building Your Own Pipeline[49]

Messer Construction,[50] a $1.5 billion Cincinnati-based company, was founded in the 1930s by immigrant carpenter Frank Messer. From its first major project during the Great Depression building the Nashville

Post Office in 1932, Messer grew rapidly in the postwar years, becoming one of the nation's leading commercial construction managers and general contractors.

Today, Messer employs 1,300 staff, including 525 craft workers, based out of eleven regional offices in Ohio, Indiana, Tennessee, North Carolina, and Kentucky. Messer specializes in commercial construction in the aviation, health care, higher education, industrial, and science technology sectors.

Messer's People-Centered Culture

Messer is well-known in the construction industry for its robust, people-centered culture, which is deeply embedded in its talent, leadership, and business operations practices. Pete Strange, former CEO and current board member, cites one of his mentors, Joe Glassmeyer, who taught him what soon became Messer's leadership philosophy: "Look for someone who is causing the people around them to get better results, make better decisions, and to think longer term. . . . They create 100 percent of the value in this world, and about 99 percent of the fun."

HR as a Strategic C-Suite Player

Messer's Human Resources Department plays an essential C-suite role within the company's business strategy. CEO Tim Steigerwald proudly offers one concrete example of how HR has become a strategic force in the face of a chronically tight labor market: "Because of the E-Verify system for immigrant workers, we used to be very reluctant to grow our Hispanic workforce for fear of disbarment. But now, given the challenges of recruiting workers, we knew we had to change—and so HR was charged with creative solutions, such as a greater reliance on workers with five-year work visas."

Senior VP Nick Apanius, who leads Messer's HR department, offers another, very personal example: In the depths of the 2008 recession, when its competitors were laying off hundreds of employees, Messer held on to its own. Apanius, who says, "I myself should have been laid off," was instead asked to take on a wide range of research and operational improvement tasks. When the economy came roaring back, Apanius and the rest of the Messer workforce were well positioned to get a jump on their competitors.

The Messer Talent Pipeline System

In the face of a chronically tight labor market, the secret of Messer's success is the crafting of its sophisticated talent pipeline system. For example, 41 percent of Messer's Operations employees were hired through *co-ops*, which are paid "work experiences" managed in partnership with several area colleges and universities.

Apanius, who himself got his start at Messer through a co-op, calls the company's pipeline system a "well-oiled machine" that allows each student to learn what kind of company he or she wants to work for while at the same time allowing Messer to learn the potential of each student. As a result, those hired through the Messer co-op pipeline generate significantly higher retention rates than non-co-op hires. Messer strongly encourages its senior employees to engage deeply with their regional educational institutions through teaching, visiting, working closely with faculty, and becoming a known presence on each area campus.

Senior VP of Operations Services Rob Verst notes, "The days of the well-seasoned journeyman showing up on our door are over. And recruiting from walk-ins, or applying through online hiring intermediaries, or randomly from the web, just doesn't work; from those sources, less than 10 percent of initial applicants even show up. Instead, we now recruit and train people ourselves."

In 2024, Messer fielded twenty-four paid vocational and high school co-ops; for 2025, the goal was to reach forty co-op hires from schools throughout all eleven of the company's cities. Widening its hiring funnel has also led to changes in Messer's recruitment and hiring *systems*: The company has now moved away entirely from online applications and toward in-person skills assessment, which brings candidates on site so that each one can be seen and assessed in person.

Widening the Hiring Funnel

In 2020, Messer doubled down on its long-standing DEI commitment. As CEO Tim Steigerwald states: "Messer is committed to leadership in creating economic opportunities for all segments of our regional communities. We believe sustainable change requires the inclusion of the entire markets and workforce including underrepresented businesses and talent from varied backgrounds. If we are to sustain growth and continue to compete in this ever-changing business environment, it is imperative that our economic inclusion initiatives continue to support and uplift our communities."[51]

Messer has continued to expand its DEI strategy to make it a central element in the company's talent attraction and retention strategy. According to Pete Strange, "Doing right is a competitive advantage. Our Urban Workforce Development Initiative (UWDI) has led to project awards that might have gone to other contractors."

Initiated during Messer's construction of the Cincinnati Children's Hospital, the UWDI is now a formal part of Messer's talent pipeline. A key community partner, Easter Seals, provides "work hardening" training for its new recruits, preparing individuals who may have never worked in *any* job before joining the program. The Easter Seals participants engage in up to ten weeks of intensive work preparation and then join Messer's preapprenticeship program.

As the program expanded, Messer hired a full-time workforce coordinator, a former National Football League player who "chases down" and supports new recruits if they fail to show up. Related partners provide a wide range of support services, including transportation and emergency funds. CEO Steigerwald notes that Messer wants and needs to replicate this model in other cities and is seeking partners like Easter Seals in those cities—but it will replicate the program internally if necessary.

Looking back, Pete Strange argues that the foundation of success in widening the Messer hiring funnel consists of four key elements:

- Engaging overt and strong CEO leadership
- Offering work hardening preparation through apprenticeships

- Supporting employees by providing coaches who are both "den mothers and sergeant majors"
- Training foremen and other supervisors "who have tremendous construction skills—but aren't social workers" so that they can support and bring out the best in their people

This formula is clearly succeeding, as Messer continues to grow, attract, and retain talent—while still beating out its competition on a national scale.

Retooling *Whom* You Hire

Just who is the untapped talent in today's economy? Even in a forever-tight labor market, far more talent is available than you might think. In addition to the workers you can attract from other companies, you may well consider unemployed workers to be the primary source of available talent—and this is indeed a large group, with more than 7.3 million Americans currently unemployed at the time of writing.[52]

Yet the unemployed do not tell the whole story. Millions of Americans are "available" and want to work, or work more hours, yet they are not officially counted as unemployed—because they are either working fewer hours than they want or not "actively looking" for a job. These are the *under*employed, and there are more than ten million of them.

One study in 2020 estimated that the number of *underemployed* Americans is more than five times the number of *unemployed* workers.[53] Another, more recent study looked in detail at untapped talent in Massachusetts and estimated that the commonwealth included more than 400,000 underemployed individuals—nearly four times the number of those officially unemployed at the time.[54]

The Seven Segments of Untapped Talent

Untapped talent can be roughly divided into seven segments: foreign-born individuals, older individuals, people living with disabilities, caregivers, young individuals, ex-offenders, and people of color.[55] These individuals possess a wide range of education and skills, yet they face barriers to participating fully in the workforce. Many untapped workers are highly educated and have extensive employment experience, either in the US or elsewhere.

When you do choose to tap this enormous well of talent, the reward will be considerable: Tapping untapped talent not only fills your open positions, it enables you to build a more diverse and inclusive workforce that better reflects the increasing diversity of your customer base.[56] That said, we acknowledge that aggressive governmental and extragovernmental attacks on diverse and inclusive hiring in both public and private spheres may have a chilling effect on your efforts, making them more difficult to initiate and sustain. We offer these approaches to expand whom you hire not as an ideological argument, but as a pragmatic and strategic response to a forever-tight labor market.

Periods of especially tight labor markets often have a markedly positive impact on the individual earnings of low-income individuals and workers of color, and these earnings gains tend to stick even in business downturns. Perhaps even more significant is that these wage gains often have long-lasting impacts on the social and economic vibrancy of local low-income neighborhoods and communities of color.[57]

The key to tapping untapped candidates is to resist perceiving them monolithically. Instead, understand the distinct work assets they offer—along with the particular challenges they face. However, many employment barriers do exist that are often common across all seven segments. These include sporadic work histories, limited formal education, and economic insecurity that can impact housing, transportation, and, in general, daily living.

These common barriers can be addressed both during the hiring process and once an individual is employed. For example, sporadic work histories can be reassessed, as we have already noted, through recasting job descriptions and readjusting applicant-tracking systems, while limited formal education can be addressed through more sophisticated skills-first talent strategies. Economic insecurities can be addressed through internal coaching support and enhanced employee assistance programs.

In addition to executing a plan to address these common barriers, it is also worth diving a bit deeper into each of the seven population segments, to better understand their specific barriers and how to address them.

Foreign-Born Workers Until the recent shift in federal immigration policy, foreign-born individuals had been the fastest growing segment of the American labor force, serving as the primary source of all job growth in the United States since the end of the pandemic (see figure 1.5). As recently as 2024, there were approximately twenty-seven million work-authorized foreign-born workers in the US, comprising more than 10 percent of the workforce.[58] Despite recent changes to federal policy, millions of foreign-born workers still remain in the US.

Foreign-born workers face two unique barriers: language and social networks. English fluency is necessary for most jobs in American workplaces. Foreign-born workers possess a wide range of English fluency limitations, depending upon their country of origin, length of time in the United States, and educational level. Estimates suggest that nearly half of the foreign-born population has limited English proficiency.[59]

Many foreign-born workers are highly trained professionals, often filling technology jobs through the coveted federal H-1B visa program.[60] Many others are well-educated in their country of origin yet face limited career opportunities in the US due to nontransferable foreign certifications or limited English competency. Notably, there are more than two million underemployed *college-educated* immigrants residing in the United States.[61] Others, due to their circumstances in their country of origin or the disruptions of migration, have both limited English and limited formal education.

The single most important strategy for more effectively tapping untapped foreign-born talent is to increase the availability of high-quality English language instruction. This is particularly true if the English language training can be contextualized specifically for the type of job for which the foreign-born candidate is applying.

Fortunately, a recent explosion of new educational delivery technologies and online curricula has occurred. This has resulted in affordable, quality, vocational English-training options, which can now be delivered at all times of day, remotely or in person, while also being highly adaptable to fit individual learners' learning styles and levels of English competency.[62]

With this leap in technology, your company can now directly provide vocational English instruction to upgrade your employees' skills. Or, if you prefer, you can partner with experienced third-party providers that are able to blend English language instruction with other skill enhancements and coaching for both incumbent employees and potential candidates.

An additional strategy specific to foreign-born workers is bolstering their social capital. When working adults emigrate to the United States, they typically leave behind all their related formal and informal networks of information and their connections to jobs, careers, and related opportunities.

Other than the few foreign-born workers who have direct immigration links to specific employers—as is the case with H-1B visas or employer-sponsored refugee-resettlement services—many foreign-born workers lack an understanding of how the industry or occupation they left behind works here in the United States. Few, if any, have American professional relationships. And in the case of many highly educated and professionally trained foreign-born workers, the degrees, licenses, and certifications they had in their native country are not accepted in the United States. This is the reason, as you make your way to the airport, that you may meet a foreign-born Uber driver discussing his scientific research career back home.

Helping foreign-born workers build newfound networks so they thrive in their new country is not a simple matter, but there are reasonable steps that you can take to help. For example, you can establish relationships with resettlement organizations in your community that serve immigrant and refugee populations, thus building a targeted pipeline of job information and candidate referrals.[63] Creating formal support within your business, such as the coaching and career ladder models that we address in the next case study, can also help foreign-born workers rebuild their networks and strengthen their skills.

CASE STUDY: African Bridge Network—the Business Logic of Hiring Skilled Immigrants[64]

Emmanuel Owasu, a Kenyan- and US-trained urban planner, so frequently encountered highly educated professional immigrants struggling to get a foothold in the American work world that he left his job in state government in 2020 to launch the Massachusetts-based African Bridge Network (ABN).[65]

Owasu emphasizes that regions across the nation, and the employers who do business there, now compete for skilled immigrants who increasingly migrate to the most immigrant-friendly communities, which in turn offer the best economic opportunities. This competition for migrant workers was exacerbated by the labor shortages following the COVID-19 pandemic. Although the ABN started its work from within Owasu's own Kenyan immigrant community, this organization now serves highly skilled immigrants who hail from many other regions, including Haiti, Latin America, Asia, and, of course, Africa.

ABN and Owasu have determined that the fastest and most efficient way to connect highly skilled immigrants to higher-level employment is by focusing on transferable skills rather than recertification (which can take many years), thereby creating industry pathways and building strong relationships with employers to help overcome social capital limitations.

ABN's model is centered around its Immigrant Professionals Fellowship program, a three-month-long paid fellowship that includes technical preparation, American workplace preparation, and a workplace internship. ABN provides intensive support during the fellowship and for three months afterward with postplacement support.

This fellowship model began in the healthcare industry, focusing on research administration positions. Additional fellowships have now been launched for frontend research coordinators and general health care, with a finance-sector fellowship currently in the design phase. Participating employers include Mass General Hospital, Boston Children's Hospital, Beth Israel Lahey, and Boston Medical Center.

ABN has achieved encouraging results with a nearly 80 percent completion rate and rate of hire into professional positions. Recently, ABN piloted a "Skilled Immigrant Certification Program" to help ensure employers that their clients can meet employers' expectations. With its long waiting list for fellowship positions and a growing list of employer partners, ABN is well-positioned to grow its model and help tap this important source of foreign-born talent.

Older Workers The ability to hire from the large pool of older individuals and people with disabilities, as well as caregivers, was enhanced by the increased variety of flexible workplace models adopted in response to COVID-19. Although many older workers took early retirement during the pandemic, many others now want to work far beyond traditional retirement age due to economic necessity, a strong desire to stay active and stimulated, or both.

Still, although they may want to work, many older workers prefer part-time positions or work that offers more flexibility than traditional employment. By restructuring jobs flexibly to include job sharing, remote, or hybrid positions, you can open this rich source of untapped talent. You also might want to consider performing a thorough review of your older worker "friendliness" via an audit available from an organization such as the Age-Friendly Institute.[66]

Individuals Living with Disabilities The number of Americans with disabilities is also increasing within the workforce, due in part to improved health services as well as to the general aging of the workforce. According to the US Bureau of Labor Statistics, the number of working-age adults with disabilities increased by 10 percent to 1.45 million individuals between the years 2019 and 2023, as compared to a 2 percent increase in the able-bodied working-age population.[67]

Although American workers with disabilities continue to experience an unemployment rate twice that of able-bodied individuals, their labor market success surged in 2023 and 2024, rising to record highs. The expansion of remote work opportunities is most often credited for this surge, the largest among any segment of the workforce.[68]

Many employers have concerns about affording legally required disability accommodations, and many have fears and prejudices about individuals with disabilities. Yet several major employers—including CVS Health,[69] John Deere,[70] and Marriott Hotels[71]—have invested substantially to recruit and retain individuals with disabilities, with outstanding results. These flexible and remote work options have proven to be a boon for hiring individuals with disabilities.

Caregivers Individuals caring for ill family members, young children, and older parents left the labor market in large numbers during the pandemic, and then quickly reentered once COVID-19 began to wane. Again, flexibility is the key to tapping this large source of talent, including remote work and creative scheduling.

On a related note, affordable and accessible childcare is another major incentive for recruitment and retention, and many employers have piloted models that directly or indirectly provide childcare services, subsidize those services, or otherwise make them a standard part of benefits packages. Understanding and responding to the needs of your caregiver employees will pay dividends for recruitment and retention, as organizations such as Listen to Your Mothers have clearly documented.[72]

Young Workers Young workers, between eighteen and twenty-four years of age, have historically faced higher rates of unemployment and underemployment than workers over twenty-four—and young workers of color, especially Black youth, experience the highest levels of unemployment of any segment of the workforce.[73]

Young workers face several major barriers to employment or full employment. They typically have less experience than their older counterparts and often have shorter-term, more sporadic employment histories. They also tend to be concentrated in lower-wage sectors and employed in multiple part-time positions.[74] These factors conspire to limit consideration by employers of young workers: They are often screened out by hiring algorithms that prioritize steady, long-term employment as well as widespread biases that tend to encourage greater trust of older workers relative to younger ones.

Fortunately, as noted earlier, online hiring algorithms can be readjusted to widen the number of younger workers you might consider. Younger workers also benefit greatly from paid internships and other pipeline models that provide work experience and exposure to hiring managers. Once hired, younger workers benefit greatly from peer mentors and coaches.

Ex-Offenders Those with a history of involvement in the justice system represent a significant pool of workers who want to rejoin the labor force but are often excluded due to public, industry, or employer policies. Nineteen million Americans have a felony conviction, and seventy-nine million have a criminal record of some kind.[75] Several states have reformed their criminal record laws and other related laws to make it easier for ex-offenders to apply for positions and be hired.

Although some industries, such as construction and food service, are more "friendly" to ex-offenders, others, like health care, have strict limits on hiring individuals with prior convictions. That said, several major health care systems and other large employers have learned ways to substantially adjust their hiring restrictions to expand opportunities for justice-involved applicants.

For example, the Johns Hopkins Health System Corporation (JHHS) is a national leader in recruiting, training, and hiring former offenders, and it trains recently released offenders returning to Baltimore for jobs in the health care industry. JHHS works with community organizations that offer housing, transportation, counseling, and other support for ex-offenders participating in their training programs. The program's participants are recruited from the Maryland Department of Corrections and Catholic Charities, screened prior to enrollment (e.g., no violent crimes, no sale of controlled substances), and must hold a high school diploma or equivalent.[76]

Workers of Color Finally, most untapped workers self-identify as nonwhite. Despite best intentions, racial discrimination continues to plague hiring and promotion across companies of widely varying geography and industry.[77]

Numerous studies suggest that automated hiring systems, hiring manager social networks, and straight-up racial biases—hidden, and sometimes not so hidden—often lead to qualified workers of color being overlooked for jobs or promotions, even when educational levels are comparable. This problem persists, despite the diversification of our population and workforce.[78]

Addressing racial discrimination in the hiring and promotion process is very challenging, as structural biases were long in the making and are not easily unwound. Still, there are proven, concrete steps your company can take to reduce racial discrimination.

For example, as discussed earlier, adjusting unnecessary degree requirements will help counteract educational attainment differentials between workers of color and white workers. Also essential is expanding your hiring networks into organizations whose members hail from local communities of color. Finally, consider "hidden bias" and related training to help your managers avoid unconsciously or consciously hiring only candidates "who look like me." (For further guidance on in-company bias-training programs, see chapter 5.)

CASE STUDY: Wash Cycle Laundry—the Business Logic of Social Enterprise[79]

In 2010, Gabriel Mandujano founded Wash Cycle Laundry,[80] a laundry and linen rental service with the specific goal of creating jobs and second chances for people overcoming histories of homelessness, incarceration, and related challenges. Today, Wash Cycle Laundry is headquartered in Lynn, Massachusetts, providing commercial and hotel laundry services to companies ranging from owner-operated hair salons to global hotel brands in Boston, Philadelphia, Baltimore, and Washington, DC.

As a for-profit "social enterprise," Wash Cycle Laundry believes that its mission and business goals reinforce each other and that its investments in people and environmental sustainability make the company a more efficient, affordable, and trustworthy provider for its clients. In its industry, Wash Cycle Laundry differentiates itself by focusing on customers poorly served by other "industrial" laundries, especially those serving hotels under four hundred rooms and businesses of all sizes. Wash Cycle Laundry is inspired by a group of similar social enterprises—such as Greyston Bakery[81] and Homeboy Industries[82]—that practice open hiring and create second chances for individuals overcoming incarceration, homelessness, and other barriers.

Wash Cycle Laundry considers commercial laundry employment to be an ideal setting for individuals facing employment challenges, allowing it to serve as a springboard for living-wage jobs and further education. Laundry jobs do not typically require customer-facing roles, which allows employees to more easily build their skills and talents as well as their self-confidence as valued contributors to the company's success.

The company's largest facility is located in Lynn, Massachusetts, and has ninety-eight employees, almost 40 percent of whom are individuals facing major employment barriers. Nearly all positions are full-time, offer full benefits, and pay between $17.50 and $20.11 per hour. The Lynn facility, with an almost entirely Spanish-speaking staff who have low levels of literacy, also provides on-site English-language-training services.

Imani Wilkes Burg, the Lynn-based social impact manager for Wash Cycle Laundry, works as a go-between with her HR team and local community–based hiring partners to ensure a steady source of potential hires. Burg stays closely connected to her hiring partners to help resolve challenges and to line up needed support for new hires.

Wash Cycle Laundry is a growing and profitable enterprise. According to Burg, the company's inclusive hiring has made good business sense. The company is price and quality competitive, but it saves significantly in personnel expenditures: It never has a difficult time filling positions, and its staff turnover rate remains under 5 percent, far below that of similar industries and companies.

According to Burg, "For those who find it difficult to land any job, our employees don't easily let it go. Most employers exclude one-third or more of potential hires. We don't. Our clients typically are unaware of our hiring policies. And we maintain high standards for quality and performance for all of our employees, regardless of whether or not they are 'mission hires.'"

Changing how you hire, and therefore whom you hire, cannot solve the underlying structural drivers of our forever-tight labor market, but it can go a long way toward expanding your own dedicated pool of available talent. And when you combine this approach with redesigning jobs and improving job quality, which we turn to in the next chapter, you can develop a powerful strategy to improve both recruitment and retention—and thus outperform your competitors in both the labor market and the customer marketplace.

3 Focus on Retention

It just makes business sense: You want to keep the workers you've fought so hard to recruit. And clearly, to retain your best workers within a forever-tight labor market, nothing is more important than the quality of your jobs. The next case study presents the dramatic story of how one large New England supermarket chain, Market Basket, survived a challenge to its employee-centered corporate culture when its managers—and frontline employees, suppliers, and customers—all banded together to save the company.

CASE STUDY: Market Basket Supermarkets—the Business Logic of Putting Employees First[1]

When Arthur T. Demoulas first took over as CEO of Market Basket[2] supermarkets in 2008, he didn't just inherit a successful New England supermarket chain; he inherited a legacy of employee-focused management. Yet few could have predicted how, in 2014, his business philosophy would be put to the test and ultimately save the company.

Before we tell you that story, here is the business background. The family-owned Market Basket chain of supermarkets was founded by Demoulas's grandfather in 1917. Now boasting ninety-five locations across Massachusetts, New Hampshire, Maine, and Rhode Island, Market Basket stores have long been known for their low prices and loyal customer base. Under Demoulas's leadership, the stores became equally renowned for the loyalty of their more than thirty-five thousand employees: "We're in the people business first and the food business second. If we get the first part right, we're 80 percent there."[3]

This is not just rhetoric: It is a business strategy that has permeated every aspect of Market Basket's operations. At the heart of Market Basket's approach to job quality is a commitment to fair wages and benefits. While many grocery retailers rely on a low-wage workforce, Market Basket offers starting wages well above industry standards. However, it isn't just about the weekly paycheck:

- *Profit sharing:* One of the most significant ways Market Basket invests in its workforce is through its profit-sharing program. Full-time employees receive annual bonuses equivalent to up to 15 percent of their salary, based on the company's performance. Part-time workers who work at least one thousand hours annually are also eligible for multiple bonuses throughout the year.[4]
- *Career development:* Market Basket hires nontraditional talent from low- and middle-income communities and, most importantly, prioritizes promoting from within: Many of its top executives, including several vice presidents, started as baggers or cashiers.[5]
- *Benefits:* The company offers comprehensive health insurance coverage and generous employer-subsidized retirement plans.[6]
- *Employee empowerment and brand purpose:* Employees at all levels—called *associates* within the Market Basket culture—are empowered to share feedback and suggest improvements. Although executives set the direction, stores and departments enjoy the flexibility to achieve goals in their own way. Moreover, associates see their responsibility as serving and benefiting their communities; they believe they are putting food on the table for many New England families who otherwise cannot afford it.[7]
- *Low prices:* Market Basket maintains low prices while offering competitive wages through efficient store layouts and operational strategies. For example, associates restock shelves during business hours, which reduces operational costs and fosters customer-staff interactions.[8]

In addition to these policies, Demoulas's personal touch has built fondness and respect across Market Basket's entire community of managers, frontline workers, vendors, and customers. Within employee circles, Demoulas is affectionately dubbed "Artie T." The results of these policies are clear: Market Basket boasts a turnover rate of just 5 percent among full-time employees, compared to the typical industry average of around 40 percent.[9]

A Threat to Market Basket's Culture

In 2014, Market Basket's employee-centric model was truly tested: Arthur T. was ousted as CEO by rival family members who controlled the board. The new management wanted to shift the company's entire business model, returning it to a more traditional, shareholder-centric strategy. That in turn threatened the stores' worker-centered culture and foreshadowed a likely reduction in profit-sharing and other employee benefits.

What happened next was unprecedented for a US multi-billion-dollar company. Even though they were not unionized, Market Basket associates—from senior executives to warehouse workers—walked off the job in protest, setting up picket lines across the entire four-state chain of stores. They were not asking for higher wages or better benefits; they were demanding the reinstatement of their CEO.

Customers joined in solidarity, spontaneously organizing a thoroughly effective consumer boycott—later termed not *civil disobedience* but *corporate disobedience*.[10] For six long weeks, Market Basket stores stood nearly empty. The company was losing millions daily.

The standoff ended when Arthur T. and his allies managed to buy out the rival family faction, returning him to the CEO position. The day he walked back into headquarters, he was greeted by cheering associates and customers alike, to whom he replied, "May we always remember this past summer, first as a time where our collective values of loyalty, courage, and kindness toward one another really prevailed, and in that process, we just happened to save our company."[11]

Coda: Nothing Lasts Forever

In the years since the 2014 crisis, Market Basket not only recovered but thrived. The chain expanded, opening new stores and creating thousands of new jobs. The company's initial $1.5 billion loan that financed the buyout was entirely paid off. Even in the face of increasing competition from online retailers and discount chains, sales have grown consistently.

Yet, despite these documented business successes, the intrigues of being a family-owned business eventually returned when the Market Basket board of directors, elected by the same three sisters who had supported Arthur T. back in 2014, dismissed him in the fall of 2025, naming Don Mulligan, who served as CFO of Market Basket for over twenty-five years, as interim CEO.[12]

Now, think back to the last chapter, which focused on widening the hiring funnel—competing tooth and nail for workers. Two points should be blazingly obvious: First, to attract candidates, the *quality* of the job you offer is your most compelling advantage; second, the greater your job quality, likely the better your retention rate—and thus the less you will need to compete tooth and nail for additional workers.

Unfortunately, there is no single objective definition of *job quality*. A good job for you may not be a good job for me. That means just one thing: You must start by looking *within your own company* at the unique aspects of each of your different job categories—and, of course, at the unique skills and aspirations of your own workers.

How Work in America Has Changed

But before you do that, it is useful first to appreciate just how much the structure of our American economy—and the structure of the US *workplace* within our economy—has changed since the end of the post–World War II expansion years. Most importantly, it is essential to understand how those changes have in turn impacted the *overall* quality of jobs in America, including those within your own company.

A Profound Restructuring of the American Economy

Over the past several decades, fundamental changes in the American economy have irrevocably altered the relationship between US workers and their employers. As dramatized by author Rick Wartzman in his 2017 book

The End of Loyalty: The Rise and Fall of Good Jobs in America,[13] the post–World War II economic expansion years had generated a mutually beneficial relationship between many US corporations and their employees. In essence, workers were offered not only relative job security but also the implied promise that as they became more productive, they would share equally in their country's expanded wealth.

Yet starting in the early 1980s, that promise soon began to erode. The chart shown in figure 3.1, developed by the Economic Policy Institute, marks with precision just when and how the promise of "mutual loyalty" was broken.[14]

That is, as the productivity of US nonsupervisory production workers increased in the decades after the war, their compensation (wages and benefits) grew proportionately. However, that relationship of mutual benefit soon drifted apart; since 1979, productivity has increased 86.0 percent, while the compensation for production workers has increased only 32.0 percent.[15]

Many of the causes of this economy-wide unlinking are obvious and well-known. They include dramatically increased technological automation, increased global access to low-wage labor markets, a sudden shift in free-trade policies (e.g., NAFTA), and the decline of private-sector unionization—all combining to encourage widespread US "deindustrialization" of employment, away from manufacturing and toward services. Other explanations are relatively hidden within what economists now call *shareholder supremacy*. That is, structural changes in the US corporate legal environment—such as weakened antitrust enforcement and lowered capital gains tax treatment—have financially advantaged shareholders over workers.

Here is just one example of how the 1980s became such a dramatic inflection point for the "end of loyalty" in corporate America: For decades, use of a company's profits to buy back its own stock had always been considered *illegal* shareholder manipulation—until 1982, when the US Securities and Exchange Commission changed its rules. Since that time, stockholders have been richly rewarded, rather than held criminally liable, when they vote to increase the value of their shares rather than invest in research and development.[16]

The Restructuring of the American Workplace

If you entered the US business world after the turn of this century, it is understandable that you might assume that the quality of US jobs has

The gap between productivity and a typical worker's compensation has increased dramatically since 1979

Productivity growth and hourly compensation growth, 1948–2025

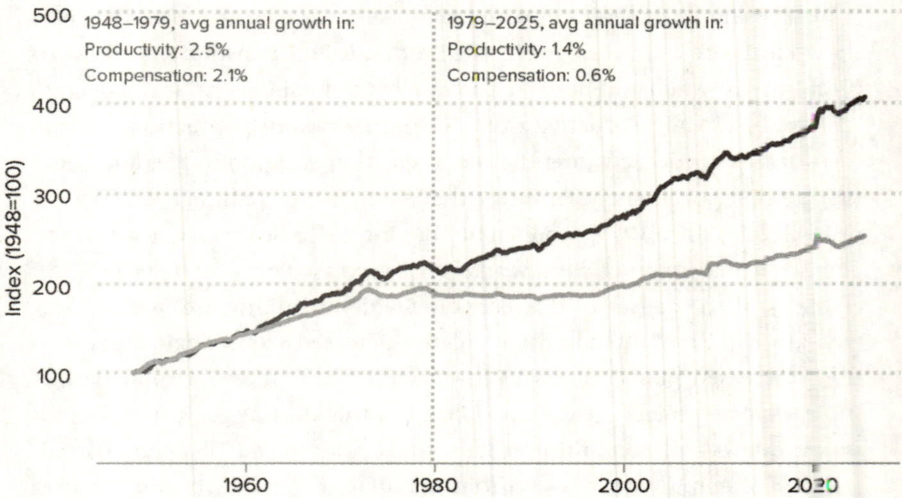

Notes: Data are for compensation (wages and benefits) of production/nonsupervisory workers in the private sector and net productivity of the total economy. "Net productivity" is the growth of output of goods and services less depreciation per hour worked.

Source: EPI analysis of unpublished Total Economy Productivity data from Bureau of Labor Statistics (BLS) Labor Productivity and Costs program, wage data from the BLS Current Employment Statistics, BLS Employment Cost Trends, BLS Consumer Price Index, and Bureau of Economic Analysis National Income and Product Accounts.

Economic Policy Institute

Figure 3.1
US productivity growth and hourly compensation growth. *Source:* "The Productivity–Pay Gap," Economic Policy Institute, updated September 3, 2025, https://www.epi.org/productivity-pay-gap/. Reprinted with permission of EPI.

always been precarious: that wages have always been relatively meager and benefits relatively limited, and that housing has always been nearly unaffordable for typical wage earners.

This is not so. Compare the job quality norms of the 1980s to today:

- *US minimum wage decline:* In 1980, the federal minimum wage in inflation-adjusted dollars was $12.29/hour—41 percent higher than today's minimum wage of $7.25/hour.[17]
- *US production worker average wage compression:* The inflation-adjusted average wage for US production workers in 1980 was approximately $24.72/hour. Today, the typical wage is just $30.48/hour.[18] Year over year, for the past forty-five years, that equates to only a *0.5 percent* increase in the average production worker's hourly wage.
- *Private sector unionization decline:* In 1980, unions represented 20.1 percent of private-sector workers. Today, private-sector unions represent just 6 percent.[19]
- *Private pension plan quality decline:* In 1980, over thirty million private-sector workers participated in *defined benefit* pension plans, which guarantee specified levels of retirement awards. In 2020, only twelve million private-sector production workers enjoyed defined benefit plans.[20]
- *Home affordability decline:* In 1980, the median home price in the US was approximately $64,600,[21] and the approximate average annual income for a US production worker was $13,665[22]—so purchasing the typical US home required about 4.7 times that worker's annual salary. Today, the median home price in the US is approximately $434,300,[23] and the approximate average annual income for a production worker is $63,398—so purchasing the typical home today requires nearly *seven times* a production worker's annual salary.

Of course, we're not arguing that the 1970s were halcyon days for all US workers, particularly for many women and workers of color. But to state the obvious, what we have today is no longer your grandfather's workplace.

If you would like to understand in greater depth the impact of this restructuring on American workers, you can do no better than to read author David Weil's *The Fissured Workplace: Why Work Became So Bad for So Many and What Can Be Done to Improve It.*[24] Weil documents how the outsourcing of business functions—think of the subcontracting of janitorial services or contracting with temp agencies for skilled nurses—has fragmented the relationship between worker and employer, "fissuring" the American workplace.

For just one example: Within the same enterprise, some staff may be employed directly by the core company, while other staff—doing the exact same jobs—are employed by a different, subcontracted company. The result does not only distance those subcontracted workers from the core company; it can also rupture the relationships between and among workers themselves. Just imagine being a line worker with seniority of a dozen years asked to orient a temporary staff person working right beside you—while that temp worker is being paid 50 percent more than you.

Job Quality from the Worker's Perspective

It is no wonder, then, that so many workers are feeling devalued. National surveys of worker satisfaction paint a far from cheerful picture: SHRM reported in 2023 that only 53 percent of US workers would recommend their employer as a great place to work.[25] Gallup's quarterly survey of the American workplace in early 2024 documented that only 31 percent of US workers feel "actively engaged" in their jobs; 18 percent are "actively disengaged"; only 19 percent report they are "satisfied" with their company; only 33 percent report they "have the opportunity to do what I do best every day";[26] and 51 percent—*more than half*—of all US workers are "currently looking for a different job."[27]

Of particular note: Gallup underscored that employees who strongly agree that they feel supported by their manager are 71 percent *less* likely to experience burnout regularly.[28] This is remarkable, given the high expense of losing and then replacing staff, as Gallup also estimates that "the replacement of leaders and managers costs around 200 percent of their salary, the replacement of professionals in technical roles is 80 percent of their salary, and frontline employees 40 percent of their salary."[29]

Finally, for a very personal perspective on the day-to-day reality of what it is like to work on the front lines within some of America's best-known companies, take the time to read Emily Guendelsberger's compelling narrative, *On the Clock: What Low-Wage Work Did to Me and How It Drives America Insane*.[30] Guendelsberger recounts, often with dark humor and deep sympathy for her coworkers, her direct experience working at an Amazon fulfillment warehouse, at Convergys (one of the nation's largest customer service call centers), and at a McDonald's fast-food restaurant in San Francisco.

We guarantee your empathy will increase for those millions of nameless frontline workers who struggle each day to meet our "I want it now" service expectations.

Outcompeting the Competition for Labor

Clearly, it is somewhat grim out there in the greater American workforce world. The good news is that—knowing how weak job satisfaction is among most other employers—it shouldn't be all that hard to compete successfully for good talent. However, that will prove true only if you focus as much of your time, attention, and resources on your *workforce* strategy as you do on your customer strategy.

Fortunately, those two strategies—competing for workers and competing for customers—need not be in conflict. In fact, as Professor Zeynep Ton at the MIT Sloan School of Management (whom you'll meet later in this chapter) reports, "The most successful entrepreneurs I have consulted to invest in a high-quality jobs system precisely because they see that as *essential* to attracting and retaining their customers."[31]

In the following case study, the 1,200-worker childcare company Little Sprouts shows what it takes to both attract and retain a dedicated workforce within a highly competitive environment. The result? In the face of an extremely tight regional labor market, Little Sprouts reduced open positions by 70 percent, increased employee retention by 20 percent, and strengthened its bottom line.

CASE STUDY: Little Sprouts—the Business Logic of Putting Employees First[32]

Little Sprouts[33] is a 1,200-person childcare company with more than thirty locations in Massachusetts, New Hampshire, and Connecticut. Founded in 1982, and later purchased in 2020 by the private equity firm Babilou, a French operator of nursing and childcare facilities, Little Sprouts is one of the largest private providers of childcare services in New England.

Recruitment and retention of childcare workers are very serious challenges across the entire childcare industry, due in large part to relatively low pay and limited benefits for teachers; higher-paying employment options in other parts of the education field; strict educational requirements; and, of course, the often-challenging work itself. Many childcare centers serve substantial numbers of low-income families, and thus their ability to pay higher wages is limited by meager, publicly funded reimbursement rates. Today, childcare workers' wages across the country remain in the bottom 5 percent of all occupations, and those wages have grown more slowly than other service-sector jobs.[34]

In 2019, the COVID-19 pandemic sent the childcare industry into a tailspin, forcing the closure of thousands of centers across the country. Later, as the pandemic began to wane, the additional costs of mitigating perceived health risks placed tremendous financial pressures on those childcare centers finally able to reopen, further exacerbating worker shortages.

Early childhood education regulations have very strict teacher-to-child staffing ratio requirements, so staffing has a direct impact on revenues. That is, if centers cannot recruit and retain teachers and assistant teachers, then they cannot open classrooms, regardless of consumer demand. By the end of 2023, the number of childcare workers still remained 9 percent below prepandemic levels nationally.[35]

Partnering with JVS Boston

Christine Trayner, head of recruitment at Little Sprouts during and following the pandemic, knew well that Little Sprouts was not competitive in the labor market and that their business success depended upon improving their ability to attract and retain teachers. As she began to develop a strategy for increasing their competitiveness in the labor market—and therefore began to build an argument for her employers back in France to prompt the necessary financial investments—Trayner came across the workforce organization JVS Boston and its Job Quality Benchmarking Index (JQBI; see the Jewish Vocational Service case study, chapter 6).

The JQBI is an online self-survey, with detailed questions in each of five job quality categories: wages, benefits, scheduling, career opportunities, and supportive work environment. A participating employer, after taking the survey for specific occupations within their company, receives a JQBI report that compares their job quality scores to those for the same positions in other companies within the same industry and region. JVS Boston then follows the report with practical suggestions for how to improve the company's job quality standings.

Trayner took the JQBI three times over a period of three years, and the survey's clear data and recommendations gave her the ammunition she needed to convince her management and corporate owners that the recruitment and retention strategies she was proposing were worth the investment. Little Sprouts CEO David Post states in a video produced by JVS that "the information from the JQBI helped to support the work we thought we needed to do."

An Entirely Redesigned Workforce Strategy . . .

With the supporting data in hand, Little Sprouts increased wages and pledged to do a full-scale annual competitive wage analysis. The company also provided 75 percent discounts for childcare tuition for employees; guaranteed paid time off upon hire, including a week's pay during closure over the winter holidays; reduced waiting time for 401(k) retirement plan eligibility, with employer matching benefits; and eliminated the waiting period for health care benefits.

Little Sprouts also instituted emergency medical services for their employees, plus free education, training, and coaching benefits. In addition, to support those staff looking to move into higher positions, the company launched a "leadership academy," developed in partnership with early childhood education nonprofit organization Neighborhood Villages.[36]

. . . and the Competitive Result

The impact of these changes on employee recruitment and retention has been profound. Thanks to their learnings from JVS's JQBI survey and consulting services, Little Sprouts was able to build a robust talent pipeline by gaining a deep understanding of employee expectations, which in turn led to a dedicated focus on job quality. As a result, Little Sprouts reduced openings by 70 percent and increased employee retention by 20 percent.

Later, recognizing that over one-third of their schools were now fully staffed, and thankfully continuing to attract strong interest from potential candidates, Trayner implemented a "résumé drop" initiative. This strategy has allowed the Little Sprouts talent team to engage proactively with interested talent, ensuring that the company could maintain a ready pool of qualified candidates to fill future anticipated openings—thus streamlining the hiring process and reinforcing a commitment to sustained workforce excellence.

With the cumulative impact of this commitment to job quality, Little Sprouts dramatically increased its competitiveness in New England's very tight labor market, with a significant, positive impact on its bottom line.

Admittedly, investing in creating a job quality *system* can be a tall order. Therefore, by necessity, your increased labor investments must be leveraged over time to maximize efficiency, productivity, and profitability. Creating quality jobs is not a matter of your playing Santa Claus, blithely passing out expensive benefits to your workers in the vain hope they will be thankful and work harder.

Instead, as CEO Drew Greenblatt of Marlin Steel emphasizes in the next case study, supporting and fairly compensating frontline workers is essential—but insufficient. To leverage those investments, the competitive employer must seek *operational excellence* by redesigning core operations, from information systems to inventory control and from cross-training to frontline decision-making. Only then will the costs of higher investments in job quality be justified, generating the efficiencies and opportunities necessary to secure higher productivity and profitability.

It is worth repeating: A well-designed job strategy does not only help you compete for and retain your workers; it also maximizes your ability to compete for and retain your customers.

CASE STUDY: Marlin Steel—the Business Logic of Worker Investment[37]

Drew Greenblatt always was a risk-taker. When he first bought Marlin Steel[38] in 1998, one of his first moves was to raise the pay of his eighteen employees from minimum wage—then \$5.15/hour—to \$8.50/hour. The immediate payoff was a major reduction in turnover. He soon raised the rate to \$9.00/hour, then to \$10.00/hour.

Today, for Marlin's 115 workers at four locations, starting wages are \$20.50/hour. Combined with Marlin's regular and sizable incentive bonus program (discussed ahead), many of the company's frontline workers now bring home paychecks of \$85,000 to \$100,000 each year.

Greenblatt is unabashed about his investment in his workforce: "I'm a big believer that you must demand a lot from your workforce—but in return, you have to belly up to the bar and pay more for really amazing talent."

Marlin Steel, headquartered in Baltimore, bends wire and sheet metal into custom steel baskets that hold *anything*—from pharmaceutical supplies to food-processing ingredients. In fact, for the first years of Greenblatt's ownership, Marlin was the largest maker of bagel bins in the US—until the low-carb Atkins diet squashed the US bagel craze and sales plummeted.

In response, Marlin had to innovate or perish, though Greenblatt admits that blind luck also played a role: In 2003, he received an out-of-the-blue phone call from a Boeing engineer who needed a custom-designed basket to hold airplane parts—and needed it, "like, *now*." That one phone call launched Marlin's diversification from standardized bagel baskets to customized, high-precision, fast-turnaround containers of all kinds.

Today, rapid innovation remains the story of Marlin's unparalleled success. For example, in 2019, Marlin's core customer base was serving the automotive and aerospace industries—both of which tanked when COVID-19 hit. "Our biggest client went down 96 percent in sales," said Greenblatt. "It was a very ugly experience. So, we had to innovate, quickly—and fortunately, we were able to pivot to the medical industry." The result: The years 2020 and 2021, instead of crushing the company, generated record revenue and profit. And Marlin has since continued to expand, purchasing four related businesses in two other locations. "We currently have the largest backlog of orders in Marlin's history."

Skills Development and Productivity

What has always been obvious to Greenblatt is that "you can't innovate unless you have amazing people, and the extra money you pay them is irrelevant." Greenblat illustrates, "So, I'm on the shopfloor talking to one of my machinists, and he says, 'You hear that? It's making a "clickety clack" sound when it should be making a "vrhoom vrhoom" sound.' So, we call over our mechanic, and it becomes a $1,000 fix now instead of a $25,000 disaster a few days from now. Sure, I'm paying him more than what he would earn elsewhere, but that machinist's unique intuition is invaluable."

Greenblatt has always designed Marlin to reward two things: skill development—particularly cross-training to perform more than just one job—and productivity.

Skills Development

From the start, Greenblatt introduced the skills matrix. He posted on the wall in the lunchroom for all to see the skills that each worker had mastered, with a formula that promised what wage bump a worker would receive for each new skill acquired: the more sophisticated the skill, the larger the bump.

Of course, in addition to the wage bumps, the publicly posted acknowledgement of each worker's newly acquired skills has proven immeasurably encouraging. Greenblatt underscores that the resulting cross-training of Marlin's employees is invaluable in spurring front-line innovation and company-wide agility: "If our folks hadn't been so versatile during the pandemic, we never would have been able to achieve that dramatic, rapid shift in our customer base."

Productivity

While the skills matrix rewards quality inputs, Marlin's bonus program rewards quality output. There are several key elements of how Marlin structures its bonuses to encourage productivity:

- *Production targets* must be clearly defined, frequent, reasonably attainable, and "close to the worker," meaning that they are designed to reward small-team, not company-wide, outcomes.
- *The size of the bonuses* must be *large*—large enough, Greenblatt says, that "the worker's spouse knows when a bonus target was or wasn't met. A little family encouragement never hurts."

Not Just Money

Yet it isn't just about the money. As Greenblatt is quick to emphasize: "You've got to genuinely care about your employees. And I don't mean just what you say, it's what you *do*. Most importantly, you've got to really focus on *safety*. When I first bought the company, I had two guys missing fingers and two others missing an eye. Today, we're constantly setting records for days without a safety incident—1,850 in one shop, 2,300 in another. Safety is where caring really shows."

Throughout his more than twenty-eight years leading the company, Greenblatt has never stopped believing in the business logic of investing in his frontline workers. "We went from a minimum-wage workforce to now having created a middle-class workforce. I'm really proud of that."

Redesigning Job Quality: Whose Job Is It?

All of this raises the question: *Who* in your company is responsible for job design? When competing simultaneously for both workers and customers, who is best positioned to understand the strategic intersection between securing your workforce and securing your customer base?

Your first answer may be your HR department—but is that really true? A nearly endless list of business management researchers, from John

Boudreau to Peter Cappelli and from Laurie Bassi to Peter Block, all critique HR departments as too often failing to play a sufficiently effective role in the *strategic* direction of their companies, distracted instead by legal compliance and administrative tasks. Within your own company, it may be wise to ask, "Does HR participate in crafting business strategy, or does it primarily hire, fire, and, in between, simply service employee wages and benefits? Does it help lead or does it just follow business strategy?"

Competing within a forever-tight labor market now demands that the design of your labor strategy sit at the center of your *core* business strategy—and that in turn requires that you do more than redesign jobs; it may also require rethinking the management structure of your company. The central challenge here is exploring how HR and operations, at a C-suite level, might interact to *drive* your company's business strategy in a way that places your competition for workers and competition for customers on a strategically equal footing.

As Jack Stack, president and CEO of the employee-owned SRC Holdings (see National Resource, this chapter) noted ruefully: "Around 2017, we saw the handwriting on the wall. We saw the shortage of workers in our companies and the challenges that they were having at home. We said, 'We need HR to be in *all* our meetings.' So we gave HR a seat at the strategy table. We even gave HR a board seat, okay? And HR started reporting directly to me, and I made sure they were completely staffed."[39]

Then Stack added this central caution: "But HR can't just be regulatory, they have to be in the *forefront* of the game—changing how we hire and onboard all our associates, laying out what our supervisors must do for our frontline staff."

Easy to Say—Not So Easy to Do

Redesigning both your jobs *and* your leadership structure sounds daunting, but we don't want to scare you away. So before taking on the broad challenge of rethinking how your labor strategy must reshape business strategy, we want to stress that even small changes can leverage sizable returns. In fact, we strongly recommend that you start with small efforts and, just as importantly—no matter where you stand in the company's hierarchy—that you *personally* engage in those initial steps.

That is, you don't have to—actually, you really mustn't—sit alone in your office and draft a five-year, comprehensive, job redesign plan. Or, worse yet, start by hiring an expensive consultant to do so. Instead, know that a simple change in hourly scheduling or a renewed focus on job safety or a greater emphasis on internal career ladders—or even a well-timed and genuine thank-you to a new employee—can be the start of slowly but surely nudging your workforce strategy toward the very center of your long-term business strategy.

First, Know Thine Own Selves

How to begin? Every industry, every region, every business, and every business leader is different. Throughout this book, we are introducing you to a variety of exemplary businesses and resources, all of which we believe are valuable—yet only some of which might be precisely on point for your particular enterprise. There is no single workforce solution.

However, there *is* only one way to start, and that is this: *Speak directly with your employees—and then listen.* As Scott Koloms, CEO of the 650-worker Facilities Management Services (FMS) company in Louisville, Kentucky, recounted to us: "We realized pretty quickly that the lens shouldn't really be what *we* think our employees need. Instead, maybe we should talk to them and ask them what *they* need. And what our folks told us is that they wanted to live healthier lives physically, and that they also wanted more financial stability. And so, that's what we focused on."[40]

The result? FMS experiences half the turnover of the janitorial industry nationwide. Locally, when COVID-19 wiped out competing janitorial services across Louisville, FMS not only survived but also retained 95 percent of its prepandemic customer base.

So, listen to your current workers, listen to your prospective workers—and, if you can, even listen to some of your former workers. Ask *them* what is working and what is not working for your customers, for their fellow employees, and for themselves. The answers to those questions will begin to lead you toward the elements that make up a high-quality job *unique to your own enterprise*—encouraging your employees to stay with your company and contributing to everyone's success.

The following case study is one brief cautionary tale.

CASE STUDY: Cooperative Home Care Associates—"Ask First; Act Second"[41]

For fifteen years, Michael Elsas served as the CEO and president of Cooperative Home Care Associates,[42] a worker-owned home care company that now employs 1,750 home care aides in the South Bronx. Michael shared with us this important lesson learned:

> With hundreds of home care aides, we often had aides "calling out," saying they couldn't visit their client because they had lost their childcare coverage that day. So naturally, management started thinking, "Maybe we should build our own in-house childcare center."
>
> Fortunately, before charging ahead, we decided to first survey the aides, to ask them directly what their everyday experience really was. We used an outside facilitator to set up several home care aide focus groups. And what we heard back was surprising: Most all the aides said, "Sure, sometimes it's a problem, but most times we can rely on our network of formal and informal/family childcare support."
>
> So all the focus groups came back the same: Our aides said they much preferred that the company, instead of investing in additional childcare services, continue to invest in—as always—more stable hours, better health insurance, and higher pay. . . . Basically, we learned, yet again, to *ask first, act second.*

Of course, you *personally* don't have to talk with every worker—but you absolutely must talk with *some*. Nothing can substitute for a one-on-one, direct conversation between yourself and those who serve your company. Furthermore, the signal such a conversation sends—that leadership genuinely wants to know who staff are and what they value—is the most powerful way for a worker to feel acknowledged as a thinking, feeling, *productive* human being.

Employee Surveys

In gathering job redesign input from employees, eventually you may decide to deploy a formal, ongoing survey process. But first, we strongly recommend that you start with informal discussions. In addition to the "look me in the eye" human interaction that direct communication engenders, the information you gain from those initial, informal discussions will help you shape a far more targeted formal survey, resulting in far more useful, actionable information.

Should you decide to use more formal input mechanisms, there are numerous companies and organizations that specialize in workforce survey instruments. The benefit of working with larger entities is that they can benchmark the responses of your company against a wide set of other similar businesses—sometimes even within your own industry. The benefit of working with smaller, more specialized organizations is that they can tailor your inquiries to your company's unique needs.

In either case, if you decide to survey your employees formally, we also strongly recommend that you work with an outside, experienced survey organization. The most obvious reason is that anonymity of response can best be guaranteed when questions are posed by a third party. Further, experienced specialists can also provide you with guidance about how poorly designed/implemented employee surveys can so easily go awry—for example, by failing to communicate with your employees the full purpose/intent of the surveys; failing to inform employees of the survey's results; and, most egregiously, failing to follow up on the information provided.

In the latter case, it is essential to credit the survey results for the ideas that are indeed implemented—and, at the same time, to explain *why* other ideas were not implemented. In short, a poorly designed/implemented survey is far worse than no survey at all.

Introducing the Job Quality Hierarchy

As you engage in those initial conversations with your employees about job quality, we urge you to avoid attempting to codify that feedback into a single, static definition of what makes for a "good job." Instead, we suggest that you start by sketching a more *dynamic definition* of job quality, one that will best fit the unique demands of your own business and industry—a tailored definition that reflects the diverse and ever-changing interests and needs of your current and prospective employees.

Beyond Wages and Benefits

As you begin to outline your own dynamic definition of job quality, what will quickly become clear is that job quality extends far beyond wages and benefits, though wages and benefits are indeed foundational within what you will soon see emerge as a job quality *hierarchy*. The value of constructing your company's own tailored job quality hierarchy is that it establishes the baseline for a continuum of change—one that starts wherever your particular company wishes to begin and will change over time as your company grows and changes.

Sketching your own dynamic job hierarchy is simply meant to open up thinking—not only your own, but that of everyone within your company—about the *countless* ways in which jobs can be improved and operations can be made more efficient and customer-focused. For example, after listening to his employees at FMS janitorial services in Louisville, CEO Scott Koloms instituted a company-based emergency relief fund to help employees facing a sudden unexpected financial burden, as well as the Working Your Way to Wheels and Working Your Way Home programs, for which FMS provides a financial match. To date, these latter two programs have helped twenty-two FMS employees buy their own cars and thirteen FMS employees become new homeowners.[43]

Once you've begun engaging directly with and listening closely to your own employees and coworkers, only then will you want to start making decisions: which job redesign models you might like to emulate, what resources you will want to access, with what workforce organizations you might want to partner, or which consultants you might select.

In figure 3.2, we provide an initial job quality template. It is more extensive than many other job quality definitions, yet it is by no means exhaustive. Most importantly, it is *not a mandate, but rather a menu* of job quality elements that may, or may not, resonate with your employees.

This template explicitly presumes a hierarchy, to acknowledge that some elements are *foundational*, such as a livable wage, health benefits, and

Figure 3.2
This job quality hierarchy is more a menu than a mandate. Not every element is relevant for every business: A quality job in a start-up bakery will be very different from one in a mature food-processing plant, which in turn will differ from a childcare center or a seasonal hotel. Workers within each of these enterprises also may well value these elements differently; that is, a good job for me may not be a good job for you.
Source: Steven Dawson, "Now or Never: Heeding the Call of Labor Market Demand," The Pinkerton Foundation, September, 2017, 3. Republished with permission of The Pinkerton Foundation.

The Job Design Hierarchy

(read from bottom up)

OPPORTUNITY

Engagement	Participation Self-managed teams Pride Ownership Representation Mattering
Acknowledgment	Internal recognition External recognition Leveling of perks
Career Development	Cross training Advancement pathways Educational benefits

SUPPORT

External Linkages	Tax credits Childcare HR services
Internal Assistance	Supervisory training Job coaching Peer mentors Team development Financial counseling
Training	Entry-level Specialized

FOUNDATION

Structure / Tasks	Communication channels Scheduling Hours Job functions
Fundamentals	Safety Fairness Respect Job security Grievance procedures
Compensation	Wages Benefits Gain sharing Employee loans Access to cash within pay period

on-the-job safety. Others are *supportive*, providing necessary elements of job functions, such as training, supervision, and access to HR services. Still others provide *opportunities* for both personal and professional development, ranging from advancement pathways all the way to employee ownership.

For your own company, as you listen to your staff over time, you will want to add some additional job quality elements, remove others—and very likely reposition some higher or lower within the hierarchy. Perhaps the best way to use this template is as a true map: In your discussions with your employees, lay the draft template out on the table and ask, "Where are we now? Where would we like to go?"

Then, with your own initial draft of a job design hierarchy sketched out, you can begin your explorations—always updating the hierarchy as you test and learn new things about your company and your employees. Based on what you've begun to hear from your staff, ask: What first small step might you take to test a new job design in one of your departments? What job redesign resources do you want to start to explore? Whose writings on job redesign most intrigue you? With which of your business peers might you want to start sharing ideas? Later, what kind of employee survey might you consider fielding?

Whatever paths you begin to take, remember where you started: listening to your employees and in turn sharing your own information and perceptions. As Lagusta Yearwood, founder of Lagusta's Cafe[44] and Softer Power Sweets,[45] told us about her experiences with her staff during the pandemic, "I feel so grateful to the staff who didn't *have* to come into work, but chose to come into work anyway, during a very wild time. It taught me a lot—that hey, I really need to take care of my crew, because they really showed up when I needed them the most."[46]

The next case study is one more insightful story, illustrating how placing trust in your employees can pay dividends in ways you can never predict.

CASE STUDY: UW Solutions—the Business Logic of Trust[47]

Paul Neumann is currently a part owner and board member of UW Solutions[48] of Louisville, Kentucky. Earlier, from 1994 to 2020, Paul was the CEO of the company, then called Universal Woods. Here, he describes how his leadership team built the company into a two-hundred-employee world leader in the manufacture of hard-surface panels and high-durability mezzanine flooring.

We Trust the People We Hire

Neumann states that the core of his workforce philosophy is quite simple: "We trust the people we hire." From that premise flows all major workforce decisions:

Redesign the role of supervisor into that of a coach

Share financial information

Build team-managed teams

Invest in everyone's education

Encourage participation throughout the organization

Neumann emphasizes:

> And for me that logic of trust should extend beyond your employees to every person who has a stake in the success of your business: customers, suppliers, shareholders, even your banker.
>
> My belief is that the most efficient business strategy is one that aligns the economic interests of all stakeholders—and you can only do that if you share information transparently across all parties—and treat each with respect. If you do that consistently enough, long enough, then those you work with every day will reward you in turn with their trust.
>
> My experience through years and years of managing companies is that trust, and the return of that trust, is incredibly efficient and productive; you're not slowed down by lawyers, lengthy negotiations, layers of supervision, or assignment of blame. And you don't have to hobble with tight restrictions the 99 percent of your workers who want to do right, just to occasionally "catch" the 1 percent of your workers who might mess up. Trust is just far more efficient.
>
> And there is one other critically important lesson about the business logic of trust: You never know when and how an investment in the workforce today might result in a business advantage later on. It's just not necessarily a linear process. And in fact, that's its real power: You're not tied up by having to justify a direct, linear ROI on every decision you make because you know that benefits will eventually result, often in unforeseen ways.

An Invaluable Return on Trust

That business logic of trust paid off when Neumann was president of Universal Woods during the Great Recession. In October 2008, companies all across the economy were laying off their workers, but Universal Woods took a different tack: First, leadership assembled the entire company—sixty workers at the time—and asked for recommendations for how to create efficiencies. One idea came from a production team member: Move to a ten-hour-day, four-day workweek, shutting down the plant for the three-day weekend to save on electrical, heating, and utility expenses.

That strategy helped, but by March 2009, business still hadn't improved. So Universal Woods adopted a wide range of additional recommendations, including reducing hours for nonexempt employees to thirty per week (though they were paid for thirty-five hours) and instituting a 10 percent pay reduction for all exempt employees.

The result: No one was laid off. The benefit: Just four months later, orders began to pick up, temporary compensation reductions were reverted, and Universal Woods was able to surge back into the marketplace far ahead of its competitors. By not laying anyone off, the company had retained not only its production capacity, but also its knowledge base within its workforce, allowing it to take full and immediate advantage of the market's rebound.

And of course, inviting its workers to participate in solving the company's challenges—and holding the community of workers together during the economic crisis—only deepened loyalty and trust throughout the organization.

Coda: Giving Back

When Neumann retired as CEO in 2020, he sold a sizable portion of his stake in the company. When he did so, he wanted to acknowledge that, to a large degree, the value that had been generated during his tenure was in fact created not simply due to his own leadership, but also due to the leadership, creativity, and hard work of all Universal

Woods employees. Therefore, upon sale of his holdings, he distributed over $12 million in one-time pension investments across the workforce. Based on seniority with the company, those employee distributions resulted in the equivalent of between four and sixteen months' salary.

Of course, the job design hierarchy is just one framework for defining what constitutes a good job. As you begin to range more widely, a great place to start is the Good Companies/Good Jobs (GC/GJ) initiative within the Aspen Institute's Economic Opportunities Program.[49] The GC/GJ initiative provides a wealth of information and case studies on job redesign, including its own working definition of a *good job*.[50]

Encouraging Employee Buy-In

No examination of job redesign would be complete without a special emphasis on ways to encourage the buy-in of employees in the success of the company—from the sharing of profits to employees having a formal voice in the governance of the company. The logic is simple: The more employees are invested in their company, the greater that company's likely success. However, though the logic is simple, implementation can be complex.

In addition to simply raising wages or distributing the occasional bonus for a job well done, there are two basic categories of encouraging financial buy-in: gainsharing and employee ownership.

Gainsharing Plans

A *gainsharing* plan is designed to incentivize productivity *without* vesting the worker with any form of ownership in the company. These plans have a long and successful pedigree in the US, dating back to the nineteenth century. Later, this strategy was made famous by the Scanlon plan, first introduced in a steel plant in Massachusetts in the 1930s. Innumerable other gainsharing designs have since followed (Rucker plan, improshare, value-added gainsharing, etc.), each using different formulae to incentivize different outcomes.

Yet across all the various designs, three criteria are universal: (1) Gainsharing is designed to reward *group* behavior, not to be confused with piece-rate pay that "rewards" just the individual worker; (2) most are not based on company-wide performance but rather on performance within smaller units (team, department) so that employees can more easily perceive the results of their own actions; and (3) most are designed to reward productivity/efficiency, not bottom-line profitability. This third point is important as productivity/efficiencies are directly impacted by employee performance, while profitability results from an array of factors, many of which are far beyond the direct influence of workers.

Although the concept of gainsharing to increase productivity and encourage company loyalty seems utterly intuitive, you might be surprised to learn that these designs also have their counterintuitive critics. Daniel H. Pink, in his bestselling book *Drive*, emphasizes the distinction between workplace motivation that is *intrinsic* (inherently self-satisfying) and *extrinsic* (rewards/punishments determined by others).[51] He cites multiple studies to document how the imposition of an extrinsic motivational system—even when designed with the best of intentions to benefit the employee—can squelch a worker's intrinsic motivation. Although extrinsic reward/punishment likely works best for repetitive tasks that are rote, it can prove surprisingly counterproductive when applied to tasks requiring creativity.

Of course, many jobs require a mix of both the routine and the creative; think of the cafe baker who each morning first churns out his quotidian cornbread and blueberry muffins but then looks forward to also creating several specials of the day, or the psychologist who specializes in providing insightful care to her patients yet also spends hours each day filling out insurance forms.

Once again, it turns out that workers are indeed complex and varied human beings, with complex and varied roles within your company. Therefore, it remains essential to first *listen to your employees* when considering the design of any sort of gainsharing plan. Your strategy will succeed only to the extent that you understand who your employees are and what motivates them.

And, as always, *start small and start simple*. So as not to reinvent the wheel, you can access guidance for gainsharing designs at a general level by consulting with national associations such as SHRM[52] and more specifically by contacting your particular industry's trade or professional association.

Employee Ownership Plans

Employee ownership plans are also designed to attract and retain workers, providing not simply a sharing of gains but also an ownership stake in the company. Note also that gainsharing and employee ownership are not mutually exclusive; many companies, such as Optimax (see case study, introduction), include both.

What is most important to understand about employee ownership plans is that their design elements are infinitely variable. They differ as to what proportion of the company is employee owned, which categories of employees are provided ownership, how shares are purchased and distributed, and what rights are bundled within each ownership share.

Transform Finance, a national nonprofit organization that advises capital investors on community-based enterprise creation, describes three basic forms of employee ownership, discussed ahead in the order of their prevalence in the US economy.[53]

Employee Stock Ownership Plans An employee stock ownership plan (ESOP) is a trust structure that holds all or part of a company's stock on behalf of employees. Shares are typically vested individually to a broad base of employees, are usually distributed at no cost to the employee (often gradually over time), and are almost always cashed out to the employee upon leaving the firm. Companies financed through ESOPs enjoy significant federal tax advantages both for the seller of the company to the ESOP and for the ESOP itself.

According to the Rutgers School of Management and Labor Relations (SMLR), there are approximately 5,800 ESOPs in privately held companies in the US. Of those, 3,400 companies have plans that own a controlling majority of the company's shares.[54]

Notably, in recent years, the number of ESOPs in the US has plateaued, likely due in large part to the fact that ESOPs, legally considered formal retirement plans, are structured within strict rules promulgated by the US Department of Labor's Employee Retirement Income Security Act (ERISA). As a result, ESOPs are relatively expensive to form and sometimes cumbersome to administer. For those same reasons, most companies with ESOPs employ at least twenty or more workers; anything smaller would not be worth the complexity and expense. Among the many highly successful examples of sizable ESOPs is Messer Construction, headquartered in

Cincinnati and employing more than 1,200 workers. The next case study offers a description of Messer's ESOP strategy.

CASE STUDY: Messer Construction's Employee Ownership Strategy[55]

The leadership of Messer Construction[56] has long prioritized a culture of inclusion, belonging, and opportunity that helps them retain the talent that they work so hard to recruit and train. Messer's managers are responsible for providing growth opportunities for all their staff, as evidenced in part by the preponderance of top leaders who began their employment within Messer's co-op program and were then nurtured into leadership positions by those who preceded them.

As former CEO Pete Strange notes, "There is an expectation that the path to leadership requires reaching out and supporting your reports, engaging in the community, and building partnerships. We reward our people for supporting our people."

Back in 1990, twenty employees bought the company from the founders and other shareholders and instituted the initial ESOP. Today, Messer Construction is 100 percent employee owned. Four years ago, Messer's craft workers, who had a traditional retirement plan, were also invited into the ESOP; today, four hundred of the seven hundred craft workers are employee owners.

The ESOP has an enormous impact on the company's culture and the quality of employment at Messer. Nick Apanius says that the ESOP creates a *shared ownership culture* in which employee owners have a right to vote on company performance, can contribute to decision-making on strategy, and have an opportunity to amass meaningful wealth.

Given their far greater numbers compared to other forms of employee ownership in the US, ESOPs have received the most research on outcomes—which is generally quite impressive: Rutgers SMLR has published extensive analyses documenting that on average, firms with ESOPs are more profitable than comparable ones and that after introducing an ESOP, these firms achieve—among other positive outcomes—increased productivity, improved safety records, and lower quit rates.[57]

Worker Cooperatives The members of a worker co-op consist of the company's employees, who own and govern the enterprise on a democratic, *one worker, one vote* principle. However, while the *governance* structure (i.e., the corporate board of directors) is typically elected democratically, the day-to-day *management* of the enterprise may range widely, from consensual to quite conventional. Usually, for an employee to become a member, he or she must meet certain requirements (e.g., a membership fee, a minimum number of months employed, etc.). In most cases, worker owners control all the company's voting shares, though external equity investment is also possible. Worker co-ops also enjoy significant federal tax advantages.

Democracy at Work Institute (DAWI) estimates there were approximately 1,300 worker cooperatives in the United States as of 2023.[58] These companies tend on average to be far smaller than companies with ESOPs—as many are start-ups, the median size is just six workers—though there are several worker co-ops that employ more than one hundred staff. The largest is Cooperative Home Care Associates, which currently employs 1,750 home health aides in the Bronx borough of New York.

Employee Ownership Trust According to the Purpose Owned nonprofit,[59] an *employee ownership trust* (EOT) is a perpetual-purpose trust that typically holds most of the voting shares of a company on behalf of its employees. The typical EOT includes a profit-sharing mechanism, some element of worker input, and, most importantly, a charter protecting the company from ever being sold to a third party. Originating in Great Britain, this form of ownership is relatively new to the US, with approximately fifty trusts established as of early 2024. Both Zingerman's Community of Businesses (see National Resource, this chapter) and Optimax (see case study, introduction) have recently deployed this type of perpetual trust.

A Fourth Model: Private-Equity Shared Ownership Importantly, a fourth model of broadly held employee ownership is emerging from an unlikely source: Private-equity firms, the quintessence of risk-taking financiers, have begun to acknowledge the documented advantages of employee ownership structures. In particular, Peter Stavros, cohead of global private equity for KKR (one of the earliest and most widely known global private-equity firms) has emerged as a lead voice in the private-equity industry on behalf of what he calls *shared ownership*.

From his perch at KKR, Stavros helped create Ownership Works, a nonprofit that partners with private companies and investors to "build wealth at work" for employees.[60] Ownership Works promotes a simplified model that differs from an ESOP in that shares distributed to employees are not considered a formal retirement investment; in exchange for this simplicity, the company forgoes the significant federal tax benefits afforded to ESOPs. Critical to note is that employees' shares are generally not provided voting rights.

In most cases, the Ownership Works model is structured as a relatively small proportion of all outstanding shares within a company. Stavros considers this a feature, not a bug.[61] His argument is that employee ownership has indisputably proven its ability to generate enough *surplus* wealth to benefit both employees and the companies they work for. Yet current employee-ownership models (particularly those structured to include a majority of the company's shares) have clearly proven unattractive to risk-taking sources of equity finance. This has contributed to the fact that the number of employee-owned companies in the US remains stalled—and so only a relatively small number of workers (and their employers) are able to enjoy the benefits of shared ownership.

In contrast, Stavros' Shared Ownership recipe is to splice *relatively small slices* of employee shares into a *far larger number* of firms—a financial model that can be made attractive to external sources of equity. As stated by Ownership Works, shared ownership models can "provide all employees with the opportunity to participate in future equity growth, creating an alignment of interests between companies and employees."[62]

The intended result is to generate a competitive financial return to private equity investors while simultaneously benefiting millions of employees worldwide. Although relatively new, this equity-driven finance model is already being implemented in over one hundred companies both small and large—from the sixty-five-worker Axis Portable Air enterprise to the six-thousand-worker Harley Davidson motorcycle company.[63]

Most recently, Stavros launched a second group, Expanding ESOPs,[64] which has the support of more than fifty organizations, ranging from Wells Fargo to the Ford Foundation. The purpose of Expanding ESOPs is to lobby the US Congress for changes in ERISA, allowing for greater flexibility in establishing more, and larger amounts of, employee stock ownership.[65]

One Very Personal Journey

If you are particularly intrigued by the concept of employee ownership, you might enjoy reading John Abrams's recent book describing his extraordinary journey in helping to transform South Mountain Company—the construction firm he cofounded back in 1973 on Martha's Vineyard, Massachusetts—into today's highly successful worker-owned company.

Abrams's *From Founder to Future: A Business Roadmap to Impact, Longevity, and Employee Ownership*[66] looks back upon the South Mountain story from Abrams's retirement perch. It then goes on to describe both the continued transition of the company's leadership after Abrams retired in 2022 and the story of several other successful US worker cooperatives, including Dean's Beans[67] of Orange, Massachusetts, and Snow River Cooperative[68] of Crandon, Wisconsin.

Along the way, Abrams describes in depth both the strengths and weaknesses of the various forms of employee ownership discussed earlier, all in the very personal, accessible style of someone who has been a very successful business leader for fifty years. His reflections thoughtfully explore both the practical and philosophical underpinnings of sharing ownership with fellow coworkers within a competitive business environment.

A Final Note: Do Your Homework

If you are curious about the possibilities of any of these shared ownership plans, it is essential that you first ask what you are attempting to achieve. As noted, the structures of these alternatives are endlessly malleable; you can create almost anything you might wish. So explore with your staff and colleagues not only your immediate goals, but also what you envision for your company *in the long term*. It is true that you can start small—for example, distributing just a portion of total shares with employees—but *any* form of shared ownership should be considered a deep, long-term, and legally binding commitment.

Most importantly, understand that structure alone will not guarantee success. Although the shape of a company's ownership structure can *encourage* certain outcomes, it still remains merely a corporate structure—a vessel that must then be filled with clear vision, a human-centered culture, efficient operational systems, and skilled management practices.

Clearly, there are many paths to walk. Before selecting a specific consultant, lawyer, or advisor (each of whom will likely have their own, relatively constrained perspective on the "best" ownership structure), it is wise to begin your explorations broadly by researching the several widely experienced resources noted throughout this chapter.[69]

Job Redesign Authors and Consulting Resources

The remainder of this chapter will introduce you to four of the country's most respected organizational strategists, each of whom starts with the assumption that achieving operational excellence—and thus competing successfully for *customers*—can only be achieved by focusing on the *frontline workforce*.

Each of these four frontline models differs; one may well attract you more than the others. For example, one explicitly encourages employee ownership, while another emphasizes training. Yet you will also see that all rest upon a single bedrock presumption: that you *must* listen to your frontline employees, for together they likely know more than you do about how your company actually functions, what your customers actually need and certainly what—for them—is a quality job worth staying for.

NATIONAL RESOURCE: The Idea-Driven Organization—Alan G. Robinson[70]

Dr. Alan G. Robinson is an international management consultant who has advised more than three hundred organizations in more than twenty-five countries. "I focus on performance excellence. Business leaders hire me to look inside their organizations to help them improve their performance."

Yet Robinson doesn't start with solutions. He starts with fundamental, goal-related questions, asking senior leadership: "What are you trying to do? What are you trying to accomplish?" It just so happens that whatever those performance goals might be, they usually can only be achieved by directly engaging the company's frontline workforce.

In *The Idea-Driven Organization*, cowritten with his colleague Dean M. Schroeder, Robinson drives home this point by arguing that *80 percent* of an organization's potential for performance improvement lies not within managers, but within the frontline workforce.[71] In such an idea-driven business, management's responsibility is to tap the unique knowledge of the frontline workforce to implement "twenty, fifty, or even a hundred ideas per person per year."[72]

The only way such a dynamic culture of innovation can be achieved is through the design and implementation of performance *systems*. This systems approach is far more sophisticated than simply nailing a new suggestion box to the wall. Instead, according to Robinson's and Schroeder's article "How to Unlock Employee Ideas to Power Your Organization,"[73] the idea-driven organization is built on six key principles:

- *Focus on small ideas.* Small ideas are quick and easy to implement, have little risk, and tend to be hyperfocused on very specific problems or opportunities unique to your own business.
- *Idea-driven leaders must be humble and improvement-oriented.* Humility in a manager means having the skill to listen to his or her reports and acknowledge that management does not have all the answers—because they don't have anywhere near all the production-facing, customer-facing information that their frontline workers do.
- *Use a high-performing idea system to manage ideas.* A *system* for capturing, discussing, and following through on ideas is essential. "Nothing shuts down the flow of front-line ideas faster than employees believing their ideas are not taken seriously."[74] The system must be sophisticated enough to handle a large volume of ideas quickly and efficiently—from origination to assessment through to implementation—engaging frontline employees at every step.
- *Realign your organization for ideas.* Traditional, top-down management cultures typically end up creating decision-making pathways littered with obstacles that frustrate bottom-up ideas. "The most challenging part of building an idea-driven organization is . . . rooting out and eliminating misalignments that are impeding the flow of ideas from the bottom up."[75]
- *Hold* ***everyone*** *accountable for idea performance.* "If an organization is to be driven by ideas, ideas must become part of everyone's daily work. And just like every other aspect of work, people must be held accountable for their idea performance."[76]
- *Train your people in how to come up with more and better ideas.* For a company to improve continuously, it has to move beyond solving the initial, obvious problems; it must get better at problem *finding*.

The answer is training: teaching all employees how to identify new types of problems that no one had focused on before, turning those problems into new performance opportunities.

Connecting Frontline Workers to Business Performance

Robinson knows directly—whether collaborating with Shigeo Shingo, the world's leading expert on the Toyota Production System, or consulting for Heineken brewers in the Netherlands, or advising Good Shepherd Community Care nursing facilities in Massachusetts—that a direct correlation exists between engaging frontline employees and improved business performance. In addition, he points to a range of third-party research that continually makes the same case: from the Gallup Q12 Employee Engagement Survey[77] to the findings presented in *Firms of Endearment: How World-Class Companies Profit from Passion and Purpose*[78] to multiple annual reports from the Conference Board.[79]

Yet Robinson acknowledges, despite this broadly documented evidence, that most US managers still look to *each other* for productivity solutions rather than to their own frontline workers. "So, they're just not looking in the right place; they've just never been trained to look to the frontlines to understand their productivity challenges."

And the frontlines are where you find not just the productivity challenges, but also the productivity solutions. "People enjoy working in environments that are creative," says Robinson. "You don't get productivity by cracking the whip and inducing stress and threatening people. You get it by challenging them, inspiring them. But talk is cheap. Designing the system for handling ideas is usually the easy part. You need to educate your managers on how to build and support that system. It is constant work and self-awareness for managers—driving ideas not from the top down, but from the bottom up."

Contact

You can reach Alan G. Robinson directly at https://alanrobinson.com/contact/.

NATIONAL RESOURCE: The Good Jobs System—Zeynep Ton[80]

Zeynep Ton is a professor of operations management at the Sloan School of Management at MIT. In a recent TED Talk,[81] Ton relates the story that inspired her to move beyond the traditional operation manager's disdain for inefficiency: She met "Janet," a retail supervisor whose pay couldn't support her family, whose ever-changing schedule kept her from seeing her son or getting a second job, and who fought chaos every day at her job created by inefficiencies, frustrated customers, and exhausted colleagues.

The central thesis of Ton's life's work is convincing business leaders to "make a bet on their people. Too often," says Ton, "managers want to fix people. Instead, we need to fix the jobs, not the people." Ton critiques the dominant financial business ethos that "employees are a cost to be minimized." In contrast, the ethos at companies with good jobs are "customer-centric and therefore recognize that front-line employees—the ones face-to-face with customers—are the ones driving differentiation, growth, and profitability."

Ton is passionate about improving jobs, speaking regularly across the US and writing prolifically. She argues persuasively that low wages and poor job quality lead to difficulty attracting and retaining workers, which in turn results in poor worker performance and thus lost sales, profit, and growth. But she is clear that job quality is not just about raising wages; in fact, she notes that just raising wages without raising productivity is a recipe for business failure.

The Good Jobs System

According to Ton, creating better jobs requires implementing a system of six synergistic elements. Although the different elements will look different and have varying degrees of emphasis in different companies, she believes that they are all necessary for success. The *Good Jobs System* includes four operational elements:

- *Focus and simplify operations:* Maximize value for customers and improve productivity and motivation.

- *Standardize routine processes:* Listen to employees' input and empower them to make improvements in customer service, productivity, and cost reductions.
- *Cross-train employees:* Build flexibility and meet variability in customer demand.
- *Operate with slack:* Schedule units with more labor hours than the expected workload requires in order to meet peak customer demand, give employees time to do their work well, and engage in improvement.

It is also built upon two overarching business strategies:

- *Invest in people:* This requires good hiring and onboarding systems, fair wages, predictable schedules, training, establishing clear career paths, and creating high performance standards.
- *Embrace the values of putting customers first:* This can only be achieved by recognizing employees as your most important resource and committing to a culture of continuous improvement.

The Good Jobs Institute

Not satisfied with writing and lecturing, eight years ago Ton created the Good Jobs Institute at MIT. The institute "supports business leaders in leveraging the Good Jobs Strategy to improve their business performance." Since its founding, the institute has worked with more than thirty companies in retail, manufacturing, health care, call centers, and many other industries, including retailer giant Sam's Club, which has more than one hundred thousand employees, and the restaurant chain Moe's Original BBQ.[82]

Ton and the institute work closely with business leaders to understand and implement the Good Jobs System, yet she appreciates that many others are uninterested or unwilling to undertake such a radical change in culture, strategy, and operations. The Good Jobs System often runs into leadership concerns that it will not pay off, based on a stubborn conviction that cutting labor costs is good for a business.

"Unfortunately," Ton notes, "we have trained generations of leaders that 'market pay' is the 'right pay' and that labor is just another input to production. So why would you pay more for something higher than the market? Part of it is how we teach and think about labor, which is very wrong. We should be asking if people are making enough to make ends meet so that they can focus on their job. For too many leaders, what drives them is not being customer-centric, but instead being narrowly finance-centric."

Structural Resistance to Change

Ton also notes that implementing a Good Jobs strategy is often stymied by siloed decision-making, especially in large organizations; this may be financially beneficial in a narrow sense, but it undermines frontline workers. She offers an example:

> In a retail environment, the merchandise comes in truck deliveries. So if those deliveries are coming from all over the place at different times, you can't give stable schedules to the frontline employees because the workload is changing all the time. So, merchandising drives the decisions of how many products you're going to have; how many promotions you're going to have; how frequently you're going to change the displays. These are functions totally outside HR, yet they drive the work that frontline employees do and how well they can work, or not.

Frontline Workers and Great Service

Ton has seen directly through her work that "there are some leaders who have a strong conviction that if we want to win with our customers, if we want to create great value for our customers, we have to have our frontline employees deliver great service to them. We have to have them do the work accurately, productively, and for that, we need to have a great team set up for success. Leaders who have that mental model look to the Good Jobs strategy."

Those leaders who are willing to follow a Good Jobs strategy see tremendous results in sales, productivity, lower costs, profitability, employee retention, and growth. Sam's Club saw a 25 percent sales increase with no additional stores. Their labor productivity grew by 16 percent and turnover was reduced by more than 25 percent. Costco, a long-time proponent of the Good Jobs System, pays well above the average for the retail industry yet has enjoyed dramatically lower-than-average turnover and superior stock performance. Mud Bay pet stores, another Good Jobs proponent, substantially increased its per-square foot sales and sales per labor hour. Cincinnati Children's Hospital significantly improved its patient outcome performance.

"Their leaders are able to imagine their own Good Jobs System and have the courage to adopt it," insists Ton. Despite the skeptics and countervailing business culture, she is committed to "making the Good Jobs System the norm, not the exception."

Contact

You can reach Zeynep Ton and the Good Jobs Institute directly via https://goodjobsinstitute.org/contact/.

NATIONAL RESOURCE: Zingerman's Community of Businesses—Ari Weinzweig[83]

Originating in 1982 as a fledgling Jewish delicatessen in Ann Arbor, Michigan, Zingerman's Community of Businesses (ZCoB)[84] has now prospered into an expanding association of twelve (and counting) food-related businesses, employing more than seven hundred staff members and generating more than $80,000,000 in annual sales.

Throughout its forty-plus-year history, ZCoB has constantly evolved its business practices while still remaining true to its fundamental "three bottom lines": *great food, great service, and great finance.* Of course, you can't provide great food and offer great service without great employees. As Ari Weinzweig, cofounder of Zingerman's along with Paul Saginaw, is quick to say, "People do their best work when they're part of a great organization."

And so, embedded within that third bottom line of great finance is a breadth of employee-centered practices, including a highly sophisticated implementation of *open-book management* (OBM). Importantly

Zingerman's central emphasis on OBM is more than simply a business practice; it is an overarching *philosophy of trust* in which financial and strategic information is shared with all ZCoB employees across each of the twelve separately incorporated businesses.

Although ZCoB's dynamic growth has demanded constant change, what has never changed is its deep commitment to focusing all business development expansion within the greater Ann Arbor community. Remaining anchored at home is in stark contrast to conventional business expansion strategies, which typically pursue either geographic replication or franchising.

As a result, one critical evolution within ZCoB has been its ownership structure, which over time continues to distribute an ever-greater proportion of financial wealth to Zingerman's employees through the system-wide Community Shares (profit sharing) and Perpetual Purpose Trust[85] (managing the ZCoB business brand) programs. Starting quite early, in 1994, ZCoB began recognizing senior leaders in each company as managing partners with a financial stake in their enterprise; currently, within the ZCoB system, there are seventeen managing partners.

The Zingerman's Story

Zingerman's is truly unique; you are unlikely to find a US business development model that is as highly articulated, intentionally designed, and consistently profitable as that of ZCoB. Yet those unique, hard-won lessons can still be valuable to other companies—not only within the food industry, but within any type of business—if applied thoughtfully. "We do share our approaches, but we always encourage people to adapt to their own setting," notes cofounder Weinzweig, whose most recent writings on the Zingerman's philosophy are found in a pamphlet titled *A Revolution of Dignity in the Twenty-First Century Workplace*.[86]

ZingTrain

Sharing ZCoB's lessons externally with others is the specific responsibility of ZingTrain,[87] one of ZCoB's twelve interrelated yet independent businesses. Founded in 1994 by Maggie Bayless with cofounders Weinzweig and Saginaw, ZingTrain trains people from outside the ZCoB ecosystem who want to learn how Zingerman's approaches customer service, employee engagement, servant leadership development, OBM, governance by consensus—and, central to all, visioning to shape each company's unique business strategy and culture.

A throughline for all ZingTrain's teachings is Bottom-Line Training, a pragmatic, carefully documented approach to training that, as founder Maggie Bayless says, "teaches employees what they need to learn in order to be successful in every aspect of their job."[88] ZingTrain's bottom-line model is intentionally designed from the bottom up ("What do I, as an employee, need to know?") rather than from the top down ("What do my managers want to tell me?").

Central to the Bottom-Line Training model is that ZingTrain's external trainings are grounded within ZCoB's own past—and current—business operational experiences. In a recent episode of the *Mike Drop Moment* podcast, Bayless described how ZingTrain approaches all of its external teachings: "We never tell them, 'you have to do this.' [Instead] we say, 'This is what we do. This is what's working. This is what's not working. Here are some things we've tried that didn't work. . . . and we hear that people really appreciate that honesty."[89]

ZingTrain's website provides information about a wide array of training and education opportunities, both on-site and locally in Ann Arbor. Also posted is a listing of ZingTrain's many training seminars and webinars, as well as the extensive writings of cofounder Ari Weinzweig, describing the theories, philosophies, values, and vision woven throughout ZCoB—including the "Zingerman's 2032 Vision" document.[90]

Contact

You can reach Ari Weinzweig, Maggie Bayless, and ZingTrain directly via https://www.zingtrain.com/contact-us/.

NATIONAL RESOURCE: SRC Holdings and the Great Game of Business—Jack Stack[91]

Jack Stack is always planning ahead—he calls it *forward forecasting*—and over more than four decades of creating profitable businesses, it appears to have paid off handsomely. Stack founded SRC Holdings[92] in 1983 when, with twelve other managers, he orchestrated the buyout of a remanufacturing division of International Harvester in Springfield, Missouri. "Since we started over forty years ago, SRC has now weathered four recessions—and we were prepared for each one. Within five years of each of those recessions, we doubled the value of our company."

Today, SRC remains 100 percent employee owned by its more than 1,700 associates, with total annual sales well north of $600 million. Perhaps that is why *Inc. Magazine* once named Stack the "smartest strategist in America."[93] Now, looking ahead, Stack forecasts an ever-tightening labor market, one that will only worsen through at least 2030. Stack minces no words:

> There will be a war for talent—not only in the business world, but across all institutions that employ people. So, you've got to optimize your workforce *right now*, because the future value of your company is going to be the talent inside your business.
>
> I'm convinced that soon companies will be valued not on an "earnings multiple," not on a "growth multiple," but on the value of their talent. So, it's making the investments in training and workforce development *right now* that is going to produce a real competitive advantage . . . and at the same time, you also have to make your business a cool place to work where people are beating down doors in order to work with you.

Core Competence

The *technical* core competence of SRC Holdings is its forty-plus years of remanufacturing experience. According to SRC, "The remanufacturing process returns a used, non-functional product to like-new or better-than-new condition. 'Reman' gives old products a new lifecycle, keeps waste out of landfills, and saves valuable resources while eliminating pollution required for manufacturing new products."[94]

Yet it is made clear, when speaking with Stack, that the *human core* competence of SRC Holdings is its employee-centered design. SRC has been 100 percent employee owned from its inception, and, as Stack notes, "When people get stock in the company they work for, they have something real in their hands, a guarantee that they're going to receive a portion of the wealth they help create." When Stack talks here about "wealth," he is talking about real money: SRC Holdings has already paid out more than $200 million to its employee owners and created over thirty millionaires. Currently, SRC's associates own over $400 million combined in stock ownership and 401(k) retirement accounts.

But employment at SRC is about more than just money. SRC also offers its associates clearly articulated internal career pathways, along with the additional training and mentorship necessary to pursue those pathways successfully. Full-time workers are provided 100 percent reimbursement to pursue additional education opportunities and receive a "total compensation" benefits package that includes health, dental, vision, and life insurance. Most importantly, SRC's leadership team works every day to create an employee-centered culture, which as Stack noted earlier, makes SRC "a cool place to work where people are beating down doors in order to work there."

Open-Book Management

The key that has unlocked this employee-centered culture is ensuring that employees have the market knowledge necessary to make fully informed decisions. The conventional term for that is *open-book management*, though SRC's model is far from conventional. SRC's OBM is not simply a passive sharing of quarterly statements with a bit of financial training on the side. In fact, SRC makes a clear distinction between true open-book *management*, which requires genuine two-way communication, and just financial, top-down open-book *reporting*.

Most importantly, SRC's OBM model requires—and rewards—a total engagement on the part of its associates. In this model, frontline teams together determine their own production goals—and decide how those goals will be met. Stack has a unique way of describing what is required of management to implement the model successfully:

> You've got to give employees the *market* information they need to set their own goals. They have to believe those are their own goals, not goals set by management. And the only way they're going to really believe that is if they see that the standard is being set by the marketplace, not by management.
>
> The biggest difference is that we bring the reality of the market to the teams. I want them to see where the markets are going. I want them to figure out how they're positioned in order to take advantage of the marketplace. And based on the reality of the market they're competing in, then and only then can they make informed decisions about their team's, and their company's, goals.

The Great Game of Business

"It's all about education, accountability, and reward," emphasizes Stack. To forge those three abstract principles into a shop-floor *practice* that deeply engages frontline workers, SRC's leadership learned early on how to frame that process into a "great game" of operational decision-making and execution.[95]

Within the larger frame of employee ownership, and provided with the financial education and market knowledge emphasized earlier, the Great Game of Business model requires the following of each employee team:

- *A critical number*—selecting a key metric that is crucial for each department's success, focusing the team on its own, self-selected goal
- *Mini games*—fielding short-term, tightly defined "games" designed to move the team always closer to achieving its self-selected goal
- *Regular huddles*—holding a brief, usually weekly team meeting to review the critical metric, hold each other accountable, and consider new forward-forecasting strategies
- *A line of sight*—always maintaining a direct connection between the performance of the team and the individual team member, to the company's ultimate success

The consistent effectiveness of the Great Game model within SRC Holdings very quickly evolved into an opportunity to share the model with others. "The Great Game of Business is our way of giving back to the larger community," notes Stack, with a good deal of pride. The Great Game of Business is now incorporated within SRC Holdings as a related consulting capacity and worldwide coaching organization. You can easily access the breadth of its resources—many of which are free—and you might also consider benefitting from its extensive network of Great Game of Business–certified coaches.[96]

Contact

You can reach Jack Stack and the Great Game of Business directly via https://www.greatgame.com.

4 Rethink Government Relations

Many of you are familiar with government relations through your affiliation with your local chamber of commerce, or perhaps your industry's business association. If your company is large enough, you might even have an in-house government relations team. Whatever your size, your company probably engages in government relations in some form, and such engagement is likely focused on the traditional issues of regulations, taxes, fees, and other related public costs of doing business.

As we've argued, competing in a forever-tight labor market means rethinking how you hire your workforce and how you redesign your jobs for better retention. In this chapter, we propose an even more radical idea: that you rethink your government relations strategies in order to gain access to more workers. To do so, you'll need to shift from playing strictly defense to also playing offense. If you do, you won't be alone. In this chapter, we will show you how business leaders across the country are organizing with other business leaders to create *employer-led* public advocacy efforts that expand the supply of talent.

Expanding the Supply Side of Labor

Whether you are turned off by government politics or are a political junkie, it's undeniable that a wide range of public policies—childcare, housing, transportation, workforce training, and certainly immigration—all have a direct impact on the supply of labor. More to the point, the more expensive, more inaccessible, or more complicated it is for people to get to work, the harder it is for you to find and keep great workers.

Your understandable response may be, "That's not my responsibility. I run a business, not a social service agency." But in a forever-tight labor market, though it may not be your responsibility, it has now become your problem. Unless our business community starts to fundamentally rethink its government relations strategies, these "public" policy challenges will continue to frustrate your "private" ability to find and keep the talent you need to remain competitive.

Unfortunately, as we emphasized in chapter 1, the media, politicians, and business leaders all tend to focus on *demand-side* factors in the labor market equation—such as interest rates and the overall business climate—most all of which lie far beyond your control. Instead, you can strengthen your own company's workforce competitiveness by focusing on government issues that directly impact the *supply side* of the labor market.

As Tom Weber, executive director of the Massachusetts Business Coalition for Early Childhood Education (see case study, this chapter) warns, "You're making yourself a target if you're not participating in crafting a solution. An exclusively defensive posture is an invitation for the public sector to assume that you'll be a funder of the solution."[1]

In the remainder of this chapter, we describe the key public policy issues that have gained the attention of employer-led advocacy initiatives.

Preparing the Workforce: Education and Training

Workforce education and training are the policy issues that most directly impact businesses and their workers. Policy advocacy includes promoting public investment in training efforts as well as support for education at all levels.

National Business-Led Training Initiatives At the national level, Business Leaders United for Workforce Partnerships (BLU), an initiative of the National Skills Coalition,[2] includes employers from across US industries who are concerned that American workers do not have adequate access to skills training. They advocate in Congress and with federal agencies for skill-training resources, digital skills training, work-based learning, and higher education. BLU also has networks in many states of affiliated chambers of commerce and business associations.

The national Business Roundtable (BR) nonprofit also includes workforce development as one of its top policy priorities. BR advocates for "reform of federal workforce programs to meet the needs of the US economy and create greater economic opportunity and mobility for American workers."[3] In addition to advocating for reform of the federal Workforce Investment and

Opportunity Act, BR advocates for reform of the federal Pell Grant program for college students—in particular, to allow eligibility for *short-term* education and training programs. Many of BR's state affiliates also advocate for workforce education and training.[4]

State and Local Business-Led Training Initiatives Granted, federal policy can be quite distant and unwieldy. If you have limited time and resources to engage in rethinking government relations, it is likely you'll find focusing on the state and local levels more rewarding. In doing so, you will find that many state business associations have already begun to prioritize workforce availability in response to their forever-tight labor markets.

According to the National Association of State Chambers, only a few chambers in prior years focused on the workforce—but now their attention to worker availability issues "has exploded."[5] Specifically, many business associations are strong advocates for their state's community colleges and vocational-technical education systems, with a particular focus on realigning education curricula toward workforce priorities.

In addition, several major companies have made worker education and training a top policy priority. Walmart, long a supporter of workforce development programs through its affiliated foundation, hosted Opportunity Summit: Investing in American Jobs in the spring of 2024.[6] The summit, which attracted hundreds of adult education providers, trainers, and policymakers, explored policy changes that can help workers receive credit for their existing skills, learn the skills they need for success at work, and more easily communicate their skills to potential employers.

Childcare Accessibility

In the last two decades, the cost of childcare has risen at nearly twice the rate of inflation, outpacing working families' ability to pay. To make matters worse, the availability of childcare slots, regardless of costs, also declined during and after the COVID-19 pandemic, making it a crisis for working families in many regions of the country and therefore a significant drag on working parents' participation in the labor force.[7]

Labor force participation data suggest that the cost and availability of childcare is a growing reason that nonworking or part-time-working parents of young children are not fully participating in the job market.[8] According to the US Chamber of Commerce Foundation, 76 percent of American businesses have experienced employee loss due to lack of childcare availability, and it is estimated that US businesses lose $23 billion annually due to insufficient childcare.[9]

Some companies have taken it upon themselves to provide childcare directly through on-site centers or indirectly through childcare vouchers and partnerships with local providers. Large companies such as Walgreens, Cisco, PwC, and Capital One have expanded their own childcare benefits. Seamen's Bank, in Cape Cod, Massachusetts, provides 65 percent of its employees' childcare costs, and it partners with a local provider to ensure that slots are available.[10] Yet nationwide, despite these efforts, only 12 percent of American workers receive childcare benefits from their employers.[11]

Some employers have turned their attention to the root causes of the childcare crisis, organizing with other employers to encourage states to increase their investment in, and support for, childcare providers. For example, Better Child Care NYC was founded in 2024 by twenty business, labor, and nonprofit organizations to advocate for city and state expansion of childcare services.[12]

"For far too long, lack of access to reliable and affordable childcare has been a barrier for families and businesses," said Lisa Sorin, president of the Bronx Chamber of Commerce. "The Bronx Chamber is delighted to support and be a member of the Better Child Care NYC coalition, which seeks to systemically address childcare equity through common-sense solutions and modifications to the existing tax credit program."[13]

Several other states have also developed mechanisms to share the cost of expanded childcare with employers: Kansas provides a business tax credit for providing childcare or subsidizing employees' childcare expenses; Michigan's MI Tri-Share program shares childcare costs between employers, employees, and the state; and Iowa created a business incentive grant that allows employers to purchase childcare slots for employees from area childcare providers.[14]

CASE STUDY: Massachusetts Business Coalition for Early Childhood Education[15]

The Massachusetts Business Coalition for Early Childhood Education[16] was founded in 2021 by the CEOs of Eastern Bank, PNC Bank, *The Boston Globe*, the Harvard School of Education, and Mass Mutual

Insurance. The coalition is an expanding group of eighty-five CEOs and twenty-two business associations focused on childcare as a workforce solution for the success of Massachusetts's families, communities, and economy.

The coalition advocates for policies and programs that make early childcare and education more readily available to Massachusetts workers; identifies opportunities to improve program access, affordability, and quality; and collaborates on employer best practices for supporting early childhood needs. Executive Director Tom Weber attributes the coalition's success to being truly business-led by multiple CEOs—allowing business leaders to study, learn, and co-design a system that works for all stakeholders while developing a narrative that is built on enlightened self-interest with clear benefits for the business community.

The Pitch

In its founding, with support from Eastern Bank Foundation, the coalition's pitch to other employers was as follows: High-quality, affordable early childhood education is important for the long-term success of *all* children. The coalition founders believed that this was a public policy issue that every employer *should* care about—and indeed, as they reached out to other business leaders, they found no one who disagreed with that initial premise. Yet the founders soon learned that employers' concerns about the impact that childcare had on their *own* workforce resonated far more deeply—and so it was toward this enlightened, far more direct self-interest that they then turned their attention.

Once the coalition had built a significant employer membership, its leaders spent more than a year studying the early childhood education system, particularly focusing on possible solutions over which the business community might have special leverage. Then the COVID-19 pandemic hit: Childcare centers closed, parents of young children had nowhere to turn, and many family caregivers left their jobs. Almost overnight, what had been a relatively abstract issue became an emergency business priority.

Impact of the Pandemic

As one silver lining of an otherwise very dark cloud, the COVID-19 pandemic also brought federal government relief in the form of the CARES Act, which for the first time in US history included significant federal resources for childcare. Because the coalition had already been working closely with the commonwealth's secretary of human services on childcare issues, the organization was exceptionally well-positioned to help shape the deployment of those new resources.

Specifically, the business-led coalition funded Third Sector Capital Partners, a financial research and policy organization, to develop a new funding formula for the commonwealth to disperse the increased federal funds. This new strategy, of direct funding for the Massachusetts early childhood education industry, was very different from the traditional system of issuing vouchers for income-eligible families—which had never fully funded childcare services in the past.

The result successfully raised staff wages and significantly improved childcare facilities across the commonwealth. Building on the momentum of its success with shaping CARES Act funding, the coalition then convinced the legislature and administration to convert the Commonwealth Cares for Children program into a permanent funding stream within the state budget.

Measurable Results

In the years following the pandemic, the coalition continues to build business and public support for a more effective, robust, affordable, and high-quality early childhood education system. The measurable result of the business community's advocacy was a doubling of the commonwealth's investment in early childhood education over a five-year period through 2024, from $700 million to $1.5 billion. In addition, the 2024 state budget included $2.5 million for a pilot program for employer-supported childcare.

In the future, the coalition will work toward additional reforms to bolster public-private and employer-provider partnerships, expanding the availability of quality, affordable childcare across the commonwealth—and, as a result, allowing more Massachusetts parents to get to their jobs.

Workforce Housing Affordability

In many high-cost states, such as California and New York, housing is cited as a primary reason that employers have difficulty attracting workers.[17] In general, the high cost of housing and high mortgage rates discourage workers from moving—even to areas where wages are relatively attractive.[18]

Although the practice of businesses directly providing housing for their employees has a long history in the US, it is much less common today. Nonetheless, several major employers have recently launched innovative benefit programs to defray the cost of housing: Amazon, for example, partners with Better.com to allow its employees to leverage their company stock shares as a down payment for a home.[19] Meta has invested more than $1 billion for affordable housing construction in the Bay Area.[20] And Dartmouth Health, New Hampshire's second-largest employer, commissioned a study to show the impact of housing shortages on both families and businesses; as a result, it now partners with local developers to build more affordable workforce housing.[21]

In addition to such company-specific efforts, many employers are now joining together in business-led efforts to advocate for greater workforce housing public investment and for streamlined housing development policies. Meta and 350 other technology companies recently formed the Silicon Valley Leadership Group to advocate for affordable worker housing.[22] The Business and Industry Association of New Hampshire lists housing as a high priority—second only to workforce preparation improvements—and cites the need for ninety thousand more housing units by 2040 to meet the state's market demand.[23] In Massachusetts, the CEOs of Eastern Bank and the Charles River Regional Chamber of Commerce launched a successful policy campaign to advocate for local cities and towns to increase housing density.[24]

Advocating to increase the supply of affordable workforce housing—through changes in zoning, regulations, and public investment—are all relatively low-risk policy positions through which employers such as yourself can have a major impact on expanding the supply of local labor. Your voice, as a local employer, will be exceptionally influential.

Accessible and Affordable Public Transportation

When employers consider transportation, they typically think of infrastructure—the roads, railways, bridges, and shipping—that are needed to move goods and services. Yet access to affordable, reliable transportation is a major reason that workers can, or can't, get to work: It is estimated that 45 percent of all Americans have no direct access to public transportation.[25] State-level employment data suggest that lack of adequate transportation is a significant barrier to labor-market participation, especially among lower-income workers. Some state analyses indicate that as many as 20 percent of workers who are not employed but wish to be cite lack of transportation as a barrier.[26]

If people can get to work on time by using efficient transit services, they are far more likely to be productive; investments in public transport that reduce traffic congestion can increase business productivity by $1.2 billion annually due to the resulting improved access to broader labor markets.[27]

Unfortunately, rural and suburban communities, and the industries located within them, often find themselves isolated from any type of efficient public transportation. Even exurban areas located near population centers—which often host large employers due to lower real estate costs—may be cut off from urban transit systems or at best must rely on relatively limited regional transportation systems.

As a result, workers living in those areas tend to rely largely on individual automotive ownership. But reliance on private automobiles has significant limitations, particularly for businesses that employ lower-paid workers: Low-income individuals are far less likely to own a car, or they may face other barriers, such as ongoing maintenance of older vehicles and driver's license revocation due to prior encounters with the justice system.[28]

Even employers in urban areas often encounter transportation-related barriers: For employees and their employers alike, many aging public metro transportation systems pose serious mass transit challenges. Just ask any urban-based employer about worker productivity following a major system breakdown—or transit strike—and you will get an earful.

Fortunately, employers can address transportation issues directly in several ways. As with childcare, employers who directly assist their employees with private transportation can provide one solution: Ride-sharing arrangements, with either autos or vans, are often deployed, or at least subsidized, by many rural and suburban employers. Where a public transit system does exist, many employers provide transit benefits, while others directly purchase transit passes for their employees.

Messer Construction's Urban Workforce Development Initiative (see case study, chapter 2) identified transportation as a major barrier to sustainable employment for the company's inner-city candidates. Messer's initiative now includes a transportation specialist, and it reconditions donated vehicles for qualified recipients. Similarly, FMS, a commercial cleaning company in Louisville, has initiated a car purchasing program for its frontline employees.[29]

Policy advocacy for better transportation is by far the longer-term, more systemic solution. For example, with strong support from its business community, Worcester, Massachusetts—a city in the central part of the commonwealth surrounded by rural and exurban communities—has operated a fare-free regional transit system for nearly five years.[30] The Worcester Regional Chamber of Commerce, which has made transportation a priority for its widely dispersed membership, calls the fare-free system a "win-win for us," and their vice president of public affairs serves on the state task force to determine how to fund transportation across the commonwealth.[31]

Ann Arbor, Michigan, implemented its getDowntown program, which provides what it calls a *go!pass* to all downtown Ann Arbor employees free of charge through financial support from the city and a ten-dollar fee paid by the employer. Businesses say that the go!pass helps them retain and attract high-quality employees.[32] Finally, many major city and regional chambers—including those in San Francisco, New York City, Chicago, and Boston—focus significant attention on public transportation improvement specifically to bolster their members' ability to hire and retain workers.

The Primary Supply-Side Labor Challenge: Immigration

It is no exaggeration to say that the forever-tight labor market cannot be solved without a functional immigration system. As emphasized in chapter 1, the *primary* source of labor force growth since the pandemic recovery has been foreign-born workers, now rising to 18.6 percent of the civilian labor force, up from 18.1 percent in 2022.

Further, as noted earlier, the foreign-born population exhibits a higher workforce participation rate than the native-born population. Lost within the political clamor over the social impacts of immigration is the reality that foreign-born workers—both authorized and unauthorized—have for the last several years supplied the fuel that has powered the US economic recovery.[33] As the Business Roundtable argues, "One of America's great strengths is its ability to recruit hardworking and skilled talent from around the world, which helps American companies to grow, create jobs, and innovate. The United States will be at a competitive disadvantage if it fails to attract and retain workers in high-demand fields.[34]

National Immigration Reform Efforts

Whatever your personal politics might be, in a forever-tight labor market, continued expansion of the US economy will depend upon immigrants entering into our country through, hopefully, some form of thoughtful, bipartisan immigration reform. In fact, many national business leaders fully recognize the importance of immigrants to our workforce and the necessity of sensible immigration reform.

For example, the US Chamber of Commerce, which strongly supported the failed 2024 bipartisan immigration reform bill, argues that "America has grown and thrived because we attract and welcome the hardest working and most talented people to our shores. They come here to pursue their dreams and build their lives. However, today's immigration system falls far short of meeting the needs of our society, our economy, our businesses, and our workers."[35]

Also, the LIBERTY Campaign, sponsored by US chambers and business associations in nearly every state in the union, calls for both strong border enforcement and bipartisan immigration system reform. Other business advocacy on federal immigration focuses on several key issues, such as overall immigration system reform, reform of the H-1B high-skill visa program, reform of the refugee resettlement system, and passage of the Welcome Back to the Health Care Workforce Act,[36] proposed in the US Senate by Senator Tim Kaine (Democrat, Virginia), which would allow highly educated immigrants who lack American professional credentials to more easily enter professional health care fields.

That said, the outcome of the 2024 presidential election has, at least for now, put federal immigration reform on the back burner as the Trump administration works to dramatically reduce or end most legal and illegal immigration channels and to deport millions of documented and undocumented immigrants. However, we can expect that 2026 and beyond will offer untold opportunities for you and other employers to weigh in on the critical importance of non-native-born workers to your own industry.

State Immigration Reform Efforts

Advocacy for immigration reform, while largely a federal issue, also occurs at the state level, and in the current federal environment, state immigration policy may take on a new level of importance. In several states with significant immigrant populations, business leaders have joined with immigrant advocacy organizations to support policies that increase the number of immigrants who can join the labor force. The American Immigration Council's Global Talent Chamber Network convenes state and local chambers of commerce from across the country annually to support immigrant workforce inclusion.[37]

For example, Ohio Business for Immigration Solutions (OBIS) is a coalition of more than one hundred Ohio businesses, trade associations, chambers of commerce, and economic development groups that advocate for modernizing the state's immigration system. Founded in 2020, OBIS released the Ohio Compact on Immigration, a set of principles for state immigration reform that can attract and retain immigrant talent and strengthen the state's economy.[38]

Changing the Narrative

Given the US population's high regard for business leaders, you and your colleagues have a unique opportunity to confront head-on the negative narrative about immigrants that prevents practical reforms from moving forward. Unfortunately, anti-immigrant sentiment has taken hold in much of our country—even though two out of three Americans support thoughtful, bipartisan immigration reform.[39]

Business leaders who depend upon and employ large numbers of foreign-born workers can play a particularly prominent role in changing the narrative, by highlighting how central the non-native workforce is both to their own businesses and to our economy's overall expansion.

Rethinking Government Relations Is a Supply-Side Necessity

We certainly understand if you are reluctant to jump into, or deeper into, government relations—that is, politics. We know you already have a lot on your plate running your enterprise, and it's quite possible that you haven't had much advocacy experience. Given the toxicity of our current political environment, the idea of gaining that experience may not be terribly attractive.

That said, avoiding the public policies that impact our workforce is a missed opportunity at best, and a serious risk at worst—which in policy circles is commonly expressed as, "If you're not at the table, you may soon find yourself on the menu."

Like most business leaders who tend to focus on practical solutions, you are in a unique position to help *depoliticize* several issues that have both practical solutions and broad public support. For example, increased access to quality childcare is both key to accessing the caregiver workforce *and* broadly supported by wide swaths of the electorate—yet it is too often dragged into ideological partisan battles. Even immigration, one of the most toxic of all political issues, has very practical bipartisan solutions that enjoy wide public support.

Therefore, we encourage you to overcome your fears, holding your nose if you must, and jump in. You and your company have much to gain, and the rest of the country needs your practical, nonpartisan, nonideological voice to help solve some very solvable problems.

5 Face Resistance to Change

As you compete for workers in the forever-tight labor market, we hope these chapters have been encouraging—offering practical examples of how others have tapped the untapped workforce, retained the workers they've fought so hard to recruit, and even reconsidered their own workforce government relations strategies.

Still, we want you to know what you're up against. Many of today's widely accepted business practices are based on old, deeply embedded assumptions that presumed a relatively loose labor market—so it should come as no surprise that when you start to challenge those outdated, unquestioned presumptions, you'll surely meet pushback.

As you've seen in earlier chapters, many business researchers have thoroughly documented that treating your workforce as an asset to be leveraged reduces turnover, improves productivity, and benefits the bottom line. The most recent research, published in October 2024 by the Burning Glass Institute, Future Forward Institute, and Just Capital in *The Competitive Advantage of the Win-Win Workplace,*[1] further emphasizes that correlation.

In fact, that evidence has been available for quite a long time. In short, the *rational* argument for any business treating its workers as valuable human beings is quite compelling and widely available. Yet as we've also shown—and particularly judging from the self-reported perspective of workers across the country—the general quality of jobs across the US economy has deteriorated significantly over the past several decades.

The only rational conclusion for that inconsistency is that rational argumentation has its limits. Logical win-win documentation may be *necessary* to change behavior, but in our own experience—and that of many other workforce practitioners—it has proven time and again to be wholly *insufficient.* Something deeper is at play. That is why we want to help you face head-on the many factors that often hinder positive change in ways both subtle and not so subtle.

Also, before we dig into those challenges, we want to acknowledge that organizational change is not only difficult; at times, it can also be quite lonely. We therefore want to stress, even if you are the CEO or another high-level manager in your organization, that you don't have to figure this out alone. For example, the next brief case study describes how one eclectic group of CEOs came together to support each other, professionally and personally, in their workforce redesign explorations.

CASE STUDY: The Learning Partners—CEO Roundtable[2]

In 2002, John Hamilton launched a new business investment vehicle within the New Hampshire Community Loan Fund[3] called *Vested for Growth* (VfG). VfG was designed to help New Hampshire small businesses expand by combining patient, risk-tolerant capital, such as royalty financing, with tailored technical assistance. VfG focused on built-to-last enterprises designed by their entrepreneurs to grow their companies through the development of high-engagement employee strategies.

Hamilton soon realized that a CEO peer group would provide an effective way to support his portfolio companies. Many CEOs had parallel aspirations—to build resilient companies while also providing high-quality jobs—yet felt isolated in attempting to achieve those aspirations. Based on interviews he conducted with a range of CEOs from both inside and beyond his investment portfolio, Hamilton invited a group of like-minded CEOs to a "taste test" meeting. What emerged in 2003 was a CEO peer group called the *Learning Partners*.

The Learning Partners Table

The intent of the Learning Partners was to create a table around which these entrepreneurs could gather for mutual support and tap into their collective wisdom. This, Hamilton hoped, would enable CEOs to share their current challenges and problem-solve openly with their peers. "Some of the most productive learning among CEOs comes from experiences that may reveal their own shortcomings," noted Hamilton, "yet that is hardly ever what is discussed at typical business networking events. In contrast, a productive peer group, built on trust, enables CEOs to share real-time problems and then benefit from each other's outside perspectives." Hamilton designed the Learning Partners based on five key elements:

- *Each CEO hailed from a different industry* so that no member competed directly in the marketplace with any other.
- *The agenda for each discussion was determined solely by the members*, with Hamilton playing the role of facilitator, not teacher.
- *Topics were based on immediate problems* related to leadership, organizational development, and high-engagement employee strategies. Each problem statement was carefully defined to help ensure resolution for the presenter and useful takeaways for all involved.
- *Meetings were held monthly, during dinner hours*, hosted on a rotating basis at the site of one of the partner's businesses.
- *Each partner paid an annual fee*, averaging $1,500.

Twenty Years of Mutual Support

Hamilton selected the initial members of the roundtable, each of whom was the CEO of a local New Hampshire business employing ten or more staff. He emphasized, "I looked for CEOs who shared a business philosophy to grow their business by growing their people. They had to be curious to learn from others and had to be willing to engage with each other without a lot of bravado."

Over time, the roundtable grew to about a dozen members, and its lasting value is underscored by the fact that the roundtable continued uninterrupted, with very low turnover, for the next twenty years—formally ending in 2023 when several members retired from their companies. Peter Lehnen, CEO of Lehnen Industrial Services, a custom machinery manufacturer, shared, "The Learning Partners helped me make transparency a defining element of my leadership style with employees and all stakeholders. This has drawn more employees and customers to us, while making us a more resilient business."

At each monthly dinner gathering, the host presented a specific "problem du jour" for which he or she sought peer feedback. Member Jeff Baker, CEO of the company Image 4, a brand management communications firm, praised this structure, saying, "The Learning Partners became a trusted sounding board, and I found it powerfully helpful to tap into its collective wisdom. What otherwise would have been threats to our survival became an opportunity to adapt and grow."

Roundtable topics included the typical issues of how to recruit and retain workers, how to build "bench strength," and how to promote an employee-centered work culture as a competitive business advantage. Yet importantly, these were discussed not as abstractions, but within the context of immediate, real-time challenges facing the host's current operations.

Over the years, the partners added other events to their monthly meetings, including social events with family members, which continue to this day. They also organized occasional overnight business retreats, at which members could discuss and learn from each other about more complex, less time-sensitive topics, such as profit-sharing models and adult learning practices.

In looking back on his facilitation of the Learning Partners over the past twenty years, Hamilton reflected: "The CEOs provided each other a shoulder to lean on and an additional approach to solving their business leadership and growth challenges. Most importantly, many special bonds were created—both professionally and socially. Those will last a lifetime."

External Resistance: Structural Barriers

To begin identifying resistance barriers, start with the external environment.[4] The US economy has long been widely admired across the globe for its sophisticated system of business laws and regulations, which provided a highly stable economic environment that attracted worldwide business investment. In 2024, *The Economist* magazine in Great Britain called the

American economy "the envy of the world."[5] Not for nothing was the US dollar the world's reserve currency.

Yet that same highly stable environment also frequently has resulted in rigidities deeply embedded within a complex web of Generally Accepted Accounting Principles (GAAP) practices, government regulations at all levels, and professional licensing rules. Despite recent institutional disruption, many of those rigidities remain, and woven within those structures are both incentives and disincentives that may hamper your efforts to widen the hiring funnel and improve job quality. Let's look at some examples.

GAAP Accounting: Rules That Devalue Employees

Particularly for larger companies, GAAP guidelines often incentivize companies to underinvest in employees and dilute the value of employee benefits. In his excellent book *Our Least Important Asset*, Peter Cappelli emphasizes that GAAP rules require companies to treat employee expenses (salaries and benefits) as fixed costs that cannot be amortized over time.[6] Such accounting rules encourage owners and shareholders to value short-term savings over long-term investments—thereby both underinvesting in the developmental training of employees and encouraging the hiring of temporary rather than permanent, full-time staff.

Government Regulations: Outdated Employment Barriers

State and federal labor regulations require that workers be prescreened for on-the-job drug impairment, which is an understandable, even essential, safety requirement—particularly for occupations in the health care, transportation, and construction industries.

Often among the many banned substances for employment in those industries are cannabinoid products that contain the psychoactive tetrahydrocannabinol (THC), which includes marijuana. Traces of THC typically remain in a person's bloodstream for many weeks after last use. Unfortunately, there exists no "current use" test to indicate THC-related on-the-job *impairment*. As a result, even if an otherwise fully qualified applicant has not recently ingested THC and is thus certainly not currently impaired, the required mandatory drug testing will likely reject that applicant if THC remains in their system.

Of greater concern is that many potential applicants, knowing the likelihood of an employment screening drug test, will not even bother to apply.

This particular THC test issue has long been a chronic, unnecessary obstacle to widening the hiring funnel. Now, however, the challenge has become acute: THC products have been legalized in many states, and thus their availability and use are increasingly widespread. Clearly, current regulatory law has not caught up to current employment reality.

Professional Licensing: Rigid Occupational Requirements

Professional associations, from physicians to beauticians, have a powerful self-interest in protecting their members from unqualified individuals competing for employment. The primary method for achieving that protection is to establish, often as a matter of state-level law, licensing and certification requirements for employment within the profession.

Although such protections are essential to ensure quality and safety for all concerned—consumers, employers, and staff alike—some requirements over time can become outdated and overly rigid. For example, consider the highly restrictive training requirements that hamper creative efforts to widen the hiring funnel: The State of Louisiana requires 1,500 hours of education and training to become a licensed cosmetologist,[7] while the State of Arizona requires seven hundred hours of formal education to become a licensed massage therapist.[8]

Within the health care industry, such rigidities have often blocked strategies to improve job quality by constricting the scope of practice of paraprofessional caregivers, unnecessarily limiting their clinical responsibilities. In fact, Florida, Pennsylvania, and Rhode Island prohibit nurses entirely from delegating to paraprofessional home health aides a range of otherwise routine health-maintenance tasks—such as administering eye/ear drops and performing nonsterile cleansing. Responsibly widening the scope of practice for paraprofessionals, as many other states have done, would both improve the job quality for the aide and increase the quality of care for the home care client.[9]

Clearly, in each of these cases, the obstacles are far larger than any one company can overcome alone. That is why, as we underscored in chapter 4 on government relations, comprehensive change efforts require joining with other employers in industry-wide workforce development initiatives that can address such powerful external resistance.

Unionized Industries

For those of you working within a unionized industry, we acknowledge one more important dynamic: Organized labor has a fundamental responsibility to protect its members—both in determining the rules for who can become a union member and in the negotiation of contracts with employers. In doing so, unions must define and enforce guidelines for their members, both to ensure high standards of training/experience and to protect their members across a range of fundamental concerns, from on-the-job safety to appropriate compensation.

At times, however, those rules have proven rigid when attempting to widen the funnel and redesign job quality. Therefore, it bears forethought within a unionized environment that employers work in *partnership* with their unions to craft creative recruitment, training, and job redesign solutions—respecting the fundamental responsibility of their organized labor partners to protect the core interests of union members.

For example, establishing a labor-management committee is one proven approach for engaging unions as partners in job redesign efforts. This type of structure is explicitly allowed and defined under the federal Taft-Hartley Act labor law regulations.[10] Creating such a standing committee provides a well-tested process that allows creative explorations of labor-management collaboration on job redesign while still respecting the requirements of formal bargaining unit contractual negotiations.

External Resistance: The Cultural Narrative

Our predominant US business culture has long been one of *us versus them—management versus labor*. A powerful public narrative endures that the savvy business manager is one who considers his or her employees a cost to be minimized: The less they make, the more you profit.

Undeniably, the self-interest of labor and management will always to some extent be in fundamental tension. The mismatched power dynamic between employer and employee can never be ignored, and this book is certainly not a call to hug each other across the negotiating table. Furthermore, you as a manager can never forget—even though you may well think of yourself as a friend to your employees—that those who report to you always remain fully aware that you hold disproportionate power to reward, punish, compel, and even terminate. As Adam Galinsky once wrote of business managers in *The New York Times*, "When you're in charge, your whisper may feel like a shout."[11]

However, what we do want to challenge here is a broader, societal message. That message—which you will inevitably hear from legal/accounting professionals, from the business media, from industry experts, and most certainly from your peers—is that pursuing an employee-centered workforce strategy is somehow disloyal to "our side"; that valuing anything other than maximizing immediate financial return is at best soft-hearted, and at worst completely soft-headed.

This polarization of management versus labor is age-old—and again, not without very real reasons of competing self-interest. Yet that polarization is so endemic to our culture that it can interfere with creative ways to compete in a forever-tight labor market. It makes it quite difficult to step back and distinguish between what is a logical tension based on genuinely competing interests and what is instead needlessly embedded in how employers and working people have historically misperceived and distrusted each other.

As you experiment with unconventional ways of responding to the forever-tight labor market—recruiting from new-immigrant communities, seeking input from frontline workers, participating in employer-led policy campaigns—don't be surprised if those who are on "our side" question your decisions. This pushback may be informal and private, or it may be quite public—for example, running up against the formal policy positions of your business associations or political affiliations.

When you do receive such pushback, it therefore will be helpful to ask yourself—and perhaps those pushing back—how much of this derives from a purely logical assessment of business self-interest and how much instead is an outdated cultural presumption of an us versus them allegiance.

Over time, as the US labor market remains tight for years to come, it is likely that even more indisputable evidence will mount, further documenting that the most successful businesses are those that deploy employee-centric strategies. In turn, we believe a new public narrative will emerge: that the savvy employer will be recognized as one who treats workers not as numbers on a financial statement, but rather as thoughtful, creative, productive human beings. The savvy employer will be the one admired for understanding that workers are just like the rest of us, seeking in their work life, as author Daniel Pink has eloquently written, "autonomy, mastery, and purpose."[12]

The following case study examines one company, Luta Security, that has directly challenged conventional business wisdom in countless ways, blazing a unique workforce path within the cybersecurity industry.

CASE STUDY: Luta Security—the Business Logic of Blazing Your Own Path[13]

You've never met anyone like Katie Moussouris, and you're unlikely to know any company quite like Luta Security,[14] the cybersecurity enterprise Moussouris launched in Washington State nine years ago.

To understand Luta Security, you first have to know what in the tech world is called a *bug bounty program*. To harden its cybersecurity defenses, a company with a significant online presence will offer a financial reward, a *bug bounty*, to any third-party hacker who identifies a specific defect in the company's software systems.

Unfortunately, the result is a Wild West in which bounty hunter hackers compete against each other to identify specific cyber weaknesses. Bug bounty hunting is speculative work that doesn't guarantee pay. Only the first person to report a specific bug is paid, leaving all other bounty hunters who performed the same work unpaid. In contrast, Katie's company employs talented bug bounty hunters under contract, so even those who lost out on a bug bounty race have a way to earn a guaranteed paycheck from their work.

Despite a reputation for being exploitative of those hackers, bug bounty programs have become a widely deployed tactic within many companies' broader cyber vulnerability defense strategies. The most sophisticated of those companies now hire third-party cybersecurity firms, such as Luta Security, to help manage their entire cyberdefense system—including bug bounty platforms designed to be more ethically structured for, and transparent to, the bounty hunters.

A Culture of Equity and Healthy Boundaries

Katie Moussouris has a long and storied history of hammering the bug bounty ecosystem into one that is both more fair to the bounty hunters and yet still valuable to the companies that must harden against their cyber vulnerabilities. Moussouris led the design of the US Department of Defense's Hack the Pentagon program, the first official bug bounty initiative ever fielded by the federal government. Before that, she led the Microsoft Security Vulnerability Research program, which seeks out bugs in third-party application code.

When Moussouris created Luta Security in 2016, she did so with the expressed intent to foster a "culture of equity and healthy boundaries" to prove that "businesses can be profitable by putting people first." Today, Luta Security is indeed a highly profitable enterprise with thirty-five full-time staff and a client list that has ranged from Zoom to Facebook to the UK's National Cyber Security Centre.

Still, it hasn't been easy. Luta Security is a *bootstrapped* company, meaning it is self-financed—competing against other cybersecurity firms, most all of which have deep pockets of venture capital funding. Being bootstrapped has meant that Moussouris has had to blaze her own path to attract and retain a high-performing workforce. She's done so in multiple ways.

Negative Workspace

Luta's full-time staff all work virtually, within a thirty-two-hour, four-day workweek, with compensation and benefits equivalent to, or better than, those of comparable staff in the industry. Yet it is more than that: Except for the occasional work "emergency," Luta's staff are expected to communicate with each other *only* during those office hours, Monday through Thursday.

The result is what Moussouris calls *negative workspace*—that is, time when she and her staff are *expected not to work*, free to be with family and friends, free to pursue other interests, and, most importantly, free to not be constantly interrupted by coworkers at any and all hours. Says Moussouris, "This is all about respecting employees, respecting their time, enforcing boundaries of leisure time. In art, there's *negative space*; it's an essential element of any art form. Well, here at Luta, we're serious about creating a negative space during which you are fully expected to *not* be working."

Temp-to-Perm Contractors

Unlike most other cyber firms, Luta Security commits to a minimum gig of at least six months for its temporary contractors, which provides a relatively high degree of financial stability.

Furthermore, rather than insisting on noncompete exit agreements, Moussouris encourages her temporary contractors to secure permanent employment with their assigned clients. Over time, that arrangement clearly benefits both Luta's clients and the individual contractors, as well as Luta Security itself: Luta not only charges a placement fee but also now has a friendly "embedded" employee with whom Luta can partner for additional project assignments.

Pay Equity

For Moussouris, pay equity for all genders and races is at the very heart of her business career. "I'm not only a woman," says Moussouris, "I'm half Native Pacific Islander." She then asks, "Are there *any* women of color founders in the tech world who've been given venture capital? If so, I would like to meet her."

Moussouris's commitment to pay equity is so deep that out of the profits of Luta Security, she has created the Pay Equity Now Foundation. The foundation urges all US corporations to sign its Pay Equity Now Pledge, which includes a commitment to audit annually all "hiring, leveling, job assignment, pay, and promotion outcomes, looking for evidence of racial or gender inequity," and then to "take corrective action to pay equitably each and every year."[15]

Respect

How has Luta Security managed to survive as a bootstrap company within a venture capital–funded industry? Moussouris says, "The fact that we're still here nine years later, still profitable, with no outside financing—it's unheard of in this industry. How have we done that? By treating our folks with respect: respecting their time; paying them equitably; and, as a leader, always, always trying to act as a role model for everyone around me."

Internal Resistance: Structural Barriers

Fortunately, you have far more power to confront resistance to change inside your own company. Yet depending on the authority structure of your organization and where you stand within that structure, you will likely discover barriers that—no matter how obvious the "right" employee-centered proposal might seem—will still take far more than a single management directive to overcome.

Some challenges may indeed be obvious, but others may be so deeply embedded in company culture—because "that's the way we've always done things"—that they at first may be difficult to perceive. In either case, it is helpful to think in advance about the *types* of barriers you will likely encounter as you explore new practices.

Typically, structural barriers are the most obvious. They may include the following types.

Stasis

Few of us like change. Even if we do, we usually prefer our own ideas about what should be changed—and we particularly resist someone else's attempt to change *us*.

The obvious antidote is to include in your decision-making those employees whose behavior you want to change. But importantly, that means not simply including staff in how to define the solutions; it starts at the very beginning, by including staff in defining the *problem*: What isn't working here, and why?

And yet first—somewhat counterintuitively—when you want to start exploring solutions, it is helpful to begin with this: "Before we hyperfocus on the problem, let's talk about what *is* working elsewhere in our organization." That approach, often called *appreciative inquiry*, is a respectful way to begin exploring any serious organizational changes.[16] By initially asking what is working elsewhere within your organization, your problem-solving process can begin on a much more positive note, by acknowledging what—and even who—within your organization has been successful, and *why*. In this way, you and your colleagues can learn a great deal about your own organizational processes, drawing concrete lessons from your earlier internal achievements to apply toward your current organizational challenges.

Competing Demands

Yes, finding and retaining workers may be a serious priority—even the *top* priority. But time and resources are limited, and you and other company staff must still meet payroll, deal with customer demands, and finish the release of that new product line. That is all the more reason to *start small.*

Of course, in considering what first small step to take, you will be looking for highly visible impact and relative ease of implementation. Given all those plates you must keep spinning, an additional helpful criterion is the sustainability test: What change initiative are you *absolutely sure* that your company can sustain over time?

After you initiate that first step, and before you start any other, *sustain* it for as long as required to reap a good portion of the intended benefit. Doing so will not only generate momentum—proving to yourself and others that positive change is possible—but will also generate lessons learned for what worked and what didn't. In short, even if you have a comprehensive *strategy* in your head, avoid the sin of all-at-once implementation. It backfires every time.

Insufficient Expertise

Implementing new employee-centric strategies requires skills and experience that may not currently exist inside your company—yet another reason to start small.

Over time, deeper strategies may well require the hiring of additional on-staff experts, contracting with experienced consultants, or partnering with workforce development organizations. In any case, avoid expecting your own managers and supervisors to know up front how to achieve that all-important "loose/tight" balance of employee support versus accountability.

For example, some managers may err on the side of retaining an old-school, top-down approach to their frontline staff. Yet ironically—and just as problematically—others may err on the side of being *overly* employee-centered, unable to hold workers accountable for their company's high standards of performance. As CEO Scott Koloms of FMS janitorial services emphasized to us, "Sometimes we have that opposite problem, of managers operating *too* much with their hearts and overaccommodating individual worker needs—which is really a disservice to both the individual and the organization. It's a difficult lesson to teach—that we're not going to be able to do any good for anyone in the long run if we can't maintain a profitable business."[17]

The answer, of course, is training and support for all your supervisory staff. Yet, frankly, some managers may never be able to adjust to an *efficient* customer-focused, employee-centric culture. Full implementation of your change strategy thus may well require the reassignment or even termination of senior staff whose worldview, management approach, or area of expertise is simply incompatible with achieving an effective balance of support and accountability. Painful though it may be, a healthy, productive work culture always requires that, when necessary, you weed the garden. When you don't, the true flowers suffer unfairly.

Finally, as we noted earlier, the central importance of developing new expertise will likely encourage you to rethink the traditional role of HR. You should consider elevating HR from a reactive, transactional department into a strategic, C-suite position within the corporate structure—one whose broader responsibility will include the development of employee-centric *leadership development* among all your managers.

Structural Incentives and Disincentives

What may well be more hidden—perhaps embedded in your operations years ago when a loose labor market was the likely presumption—are structural elements that at any moment can threaten to trip up your workforce change initiatives. Earlier, in chapter 2, we highlighted the anachronistic recruitment practice of requiring overly restrictive, irrelevant educational credentials. Similarly, there may well be outdated structural practices *within* your organization that hamper the redesign of quality jobs, as we'll look at next.

Hesitation to Promote from Within

One questionable *recruitment* practice—that is, primarily poaching senior employees from competing companies to fill high-skilled positions—can also have a very negative impact on a company's job quality *retention* strategies: When high-level positions are constantly filled from the outside, the unintended result is that no career ladder is built inside the company for your own aspiring employees. Your best workers have no way to go up, so they either stagnate below or head out the door.

Financial Incentives for Managers That Minimize Current Labor Costs

Many companies pay their managers using a blend of a base salary plus incentives. Those incentives vary, depending on a variety of factors, such as the type of industry, the responsibilities of the manager, and the size of the company.

Such manager performance incentives are typically calculated using a numerical formula, usually assessed each fiscal quarter. One typical factor in that formula is the ratio of quarterly labor costs to sales: the lower that ratio, the larger the manager's incentive pay. At first glance, that incentive may appear quite rational; both the manager and the company are gaining an immediate financial reward for keeping costs low.

Yet a focus on short-term, quarterly results can also discourage managers—in direct financial terms, and even at risk of losing their jobs—by urging them away from investing company resources *now* in job quality improvements that might well generate far greater financial returns *later*. Criticism of these short-term incentives have for years ranged widely, from author Robert Slater's critique of CEO Jack Welch's uncompromising "rank and yank" management philosophy at General Electric[18] to author Jessica Bruder's own personal experiences working at the national commerce company Amazon.[19]

In contrast, Pete Strange, chairman emeritus of the employee-owned, billion-dollar Messer Construction company, has always structured his managerial incentives in terms of their *long-term impact*, often saying, "What we've succeeded in building here is a 'get rich slow' enterprise."[20]

Short-Term Incentives of Any Type

The short-term managerial compensation formula just described is one example of a hidden structural bias. In fact, nearly *any* structural bias that prioritizes immediate over long-term financial gain will tend to discourage investment in new job quality retention strategies.

For a second example: The most obvious long-term investment strategy to build a resilient workforce is on-the-job training. The payoff for that investment, when designed well, can generate value year after year after year. Yet according to a recent survey of US corporations, investment levels in employee training and development *decreased* from $101.6 billion in 2022 to $98.0 billion in 2024.[21] Again, this bias may have made sense in an economy in which skilled labor is plentiful, but in a forever-tight labor market, developing your company's own expertise, knowledge, and relationships will become ever more essential.

Distance from the Front Lines

Finally, it is worth noting that the bias toward rewarding short-term financial return over long-term investment tends to increase proportional to the distance of the decision-maker from the front line. The more distant the decision-maker, the more he or she will make judgments valuing numbers over all other factors—if only because numbers are typically all they have to work with. This critique of the dehumanizing distance between the decision-maker and frontline operations has been widely noted, dating at least as far back as Jeffrey Pfeffer's 1998 book *The Human Equation: Building Profits by Putting People First.*[22]

As we described in more detail in chapter 3, the only effective answer to counter this *distance bias* is structural: building bottom-up *communication channels* at the front lines that will reach all the way up to the decision-makers, no matter how distant. Even more powerful is the redesign of frontline, operational decision-making *structures* that, at minimum, ensure the autonomy of decision-making as close to the front lines as possible. More powerful still is structuring real input into direct *corporate decision-making governance*—such as worker councils, labor/management committees, and various forms of employee ownership (see Encouraging Employee Buy-In in chapter 3).

Internal Resistance: Organizational Power Dynamics

No matter where any one of us stands within the workplace hierarchy, each of us is only human, with all the typical, daily concerns we constantly carry inside us about our authority, our responsibilities, our pride—and our status vis-à-vis our coworkers. When asked to change, a natural first question is always, "How will this impact *me*—and what will *others* think?"

Ironically, a classic error in efforts to redesign frontline jobs has been to focus exclusively on how such redesign efforts will impact the frontline workers themselves—forgetting that such efforts also directly impact others, particularly the middle managers who supervise those workers. Initial resistance from middle managers is sometimes expressed explicitly—but more often it is expressed in passively resistant ways that may be difficult to detect. Whether articulated directly or indirectly, that resistance derives from a range of understandable, very human concerns, including the following:

- *Loss of power:* "You want me to give more autonomy to my line workers? But I'm the person who makes decisions in this department. That's my job. That's my responsibility."
- *Fear of making a mistake or appearing foolish:* "If this goes wrong, I'll be the one blamed—and I'll probably be the one who has to clean up the mess afterward. And if it goes well, hey, will that mean I've been doing things wrong all these years?"
- *Loss of peer respect:* "None of my colleagues in our industry is making these kinds of changes. My friends will think I'm getting soft—or maybe just getting shafted."

These entirely rational reactions to workforce redesign among middle managers are the reason that the forewarning to *make sure you get buy-in at the top* is always necessary—yet never sufficient. Particularly when rethinking the design of frontline positions, it is essential to engage, from the very beginning, *all* elements of the management structure that surround those jobs. And as noted earlier, this engagement requires starting at the very beginning—engaging with all staff first to define the *problem* to be solved, not just the solution.

Rarely Acknowledged: Distinctions of Class

The work culture within our organizations is inescapably reflective of that within our greater US society, and our society remains far from perfect in terms of how people of different genders, races, ages, and even appearances perceive and treat each other.

Among all our differences, one distinction exists that is rarely publicly acknowledged, and this is the hierarchy of class. This is particularly ironic as class is essentially an *economic* sorting of a person's status within our society, and it is within our own businesses that individuals are *literally* sorted according to their economic status: owner, CEO, senior management, middle management, line worker, and so on.

We all have preconceived assumptions about how these differences of class play out among us—or, in more general terms, what is each person's *status*, including our own, within the hierarchy of our organization. Certainly, those presumptions can suddenly be deeply shaken when an organization starts to consider redesigning itself.

For example, a line worker who has worked her way up the ranks to become a supervisor may be hypersensitive to now wanting to be perceived—by everyone in the organization—as a member of the managerial class, not "simply" a worker. That desire to be recognized for her new status will influence who she sits with for lunch, how she talks to her former frontline colleagues, and, in this case, how she might react to a required change toward, say, creating a new team-based decision-making structure.

In another example, a manager who worked hard to gain his business degree might question the decision-making capacity of those on the front lines who have "only" a high school diploma or GED certificate. Yet another may simply prejudge coworkers based on what part of town they grew up in. In short, the more we might presume the capabilities of others based on any one of these surface distinctions, the more resistant we may be—either consciously or unconsciously—when confronted by the power dynamics of changes in decision-making and autonomy.

If you are curious about how status impacts each of us here in America, including within your own organization, you can do no better than reading a deeply insightful book by Heather McGhee, *The Sum of Us: What Racism Costs Everyone and How We Can Prosper Together.*[23] Although explicitly addressed to America's racial divide, McGhee brilliantly approaches that dynamic by exploring the broader, inescapably human concept of *status*—"Who am I in relation to others?"—a sensitivity that each one of us will immediately recognize within ourselves, no matter what our color or gender or class.

Not to Be Taken Lightly

Finally, we want to acknowledge that any decision to confront explicitly this very human resistance to organizational change is a fraught one, never to be taken lightly. Recent studies have raised questions about the effectiveness of *diversity training*[24]—which is not to say that such training cannot have a positive impact, but it does suggest how difficult it may be to identify truly skilled organizational interventions.

Even among those interventions, our direct experience has shown how they rarely emphasize biases based on perceptions of class, focusing instead primarily on race and gender. Of great concern is that a poorly designed intervention can actually cause *added* disruptions within an organization, further increasing distrust among colleagues and making matters even worse.

At some point in your organization's journey, you may well have built enough company-wide self-knowledge and trust to engage in such training, and we encourage you to do so. In any case, however, when *overt instances* of bias arise in the workplace, confronting head-on such occurrences is essential if you ever hope to create a safe workplace culture.

At minimum, it is essential to acknowledge that biases and prejudices are endemic within all of us and that their presence—whether hidden or explicit—is always at play to some extent, especially when undertaking any change that may threaten a staff person's status or sense of self. Constant awareness of the *likelihood* of prejudgment will better prepare you and your colleagues to confront it directly whenever, and however, it does arise. As we have noted, it is surely most likely to arise when organizational change is introduced.

A Look in the Mirror

Finally, facing resistance of any kind—whether internal or external, structural or power-based, explicit or implicit—will require on your part exceptional patience, empathy, and creativity. Even more importantly, it requires courage, for you will likely discover that resistance exists within yourself as well, stemming from your own long-held practices, beliefs, and presumptions—and even your own implicit biases about what others are capable of. Change, as always, starts from within.

6 You Are Not Alone

As you've read the previous chapters, you might have thought, "What am I getting myself into?" Even when starting with small steps, tapping untapped talent isn't easy, and redesigning your jobs to retain your employees is no easier.

The good news is that you are not alone. There are organizations out there with the know-how, experience, and tools to help. They are not always easy to find, and some are better than others. So in this chapter, we will provide some clear advice from your peers who have built strong workforce partnerships—as well as from our own experience—to save you time, reduce your frustration, and increase your success. We'll also give you examples of leading workforce organizations you may find in your own community or industry.

What Is a Workforce Partnership Organization?

The workforce organizations we describe ahead typically play the role of an *intermediary*, or broker, between untapped sources of labor and the companies that employ them. They can be nonprofit, public, or for-profit entities, and they differ from conventional staffing agencies in that the best of them have deep roots in their communities—providing stronger connections to, and thus understanding of, nontraditional workers.

In addition, they tend to offer those nontraditional workers a range of *wraparound* services, designed to overcome employment barriers such as language limitations, limited work skills, and access to transportation. And finally, the best workforce partners provide, in close coordination with employers, ongoing support to workers even after employment.

Examples of these workforce partners, which we describe in detail ahead, include community colleges, career and technical education high schools, community-based workforce intermediaries, union-sponsored education and training affiliates, and public workforce agencies.

Why Workforce Partnerships?

Finding and developing workforce partnerships is not that different from any other vendor relationship: You source your materials from trusted suppliers; you contract for many kinds of technology, operational, and financial services; and you likely rely on traditional workforce vendors such as staffing firms, search firms, or outsourced HR services.

Of course, you can always go it alone in tapping untapped talent or improving job quality, and in some cases that will make complete sense. But competing in a forever-tight job market is truly challenging, and great workforce partners have relationships, experiences, and tools that can make your job far easier. Although many of your competitors will continue to rely on traditional methods—like securing "plug-and-play" talent by poaching from you and other competitors—they will likely continue to experience frustration and open positions. You, however, can forge your own path with an entirely different set of workforce partners and, in doing so, thrive within the new economic reality.

Let's examine several compelling reasons to consider developing tailored workforce partnerships.

Direct Pipelines to Untapped Workers

Great workforce partnerships excel at connecting employers directly with the untapped workforce. They know how to engage both sides of the labor market: understanding and reaching both traditional and nontraditional workers, while at the same time servicing the hiring and retention needs of employers. Some workforce organizations have focused expertise in a single segment of untapped talent—centered on either the type of individual or the type of industry—but many serve multiple populations and industries with equal expertise.

As we highlighted in chapter 2, despite recent changes in federal policies, immigrants still remain one of the largest sources of untapped talent—and each immigrant community has its own language, institutions, and social networks. Many great workforce partners have deep roots in immigrant communities—because they themselves come from those communities. They are part of the landscape, directly connected to local immigrant churches, social clubs, and human service organizations. Other great workforce partners target key segments of untapped talent such as "opportunity youth," people living with disabilities, and justice-involved individuals, each of whom has their own social networks as well as their own unique barriers to successful employment.

CASE STUDY: Jaspen Group—Employing Workers from the Haitian Community[1]

Moise Duge first arrived in the US from Haiti in 1997, settling with family in South Florida when he was eleven years old. After years of teaching and supporting youth in the Miami-Dade County education system as part of its Exceptional Educator program, Duge moved to the Indianapolis, Indiana, area in 2018—just before the COVID-19 pandemic hit. There, he started volunteering with the Haitian Association of Indiana as its public relations representative.

In central Indiana, Duge joined a relatively recent community of Haitian families drawn to the auto manufacturing and warehousing industries that at that time were desperately looking for workers to fill frontline positions. But in 2019, many of those same workers were suddenly without jobs. "And keep in mind," notes Duge, "these are folks who have families back home in Haiti that they have to take care of as well."

In January 2020, Duge volunteered to become the executive director of the Haitian Association of Indiana. Haitian families initially approached the association looking for services, said Duge: "When the pandemic came, we started a food-distribution program to help families. But we quickly realized 'okay, this is not sustainable.' That's how we ended up starting the staffing business—because once you can help somebody find work, then they have money in their own pocket, and they can begin to take care of themselves." With that, the for-profit Jaspen Group staffing and training agency was born, with Moise Duge as founding CEO.

Today, the Jaspen Group remains deeply embedded within the Haitian community, now with offices in West Indianapolis, East Indianapolis, Evansville, and Washington, Indiana, as well as Lexington, Kentucky. Serving a range of employers within those regions, Jaspen provides workforce services that include temp, temp-to-hire, and direct-hire placements, as well as drug screening, background checks, and payroll services.

Transportation and Housing Challenges in the Rural Midwest

What is particularly important to understand about Jaspen's Midwest service area is that much of the region is quite rural, with an aging workforce still reeling from the opioid crisis. Jaspen learned early on that the employers who had the greatest recruitment and retention problems were the most rural, situated farthest from population centers and thus farthest from potential workers.

This meant that Jaspen could be of little help to employers if it only functioned as a traditional staffing agency. Yes, it had deep roots in the community, with many families looking for work; and yes, it knew many employers who needed plenty of workers—but the agency couldn't connect the two unless Jaspen could figure out ways to craft innovative transportation and housing solutions.

So, that's what it did, says Duge: "We partnered with local agencies to provide passenger vans to get our clients to their jobs, and temporary housing for others until they could transition into permanent housing nearer their employment. At our peak right in the aftermath of the pandemic, we had over two hundred temporary beds all over the Midwest, helping our people slowly transition into permanent housing to become part of the greater fabric of the community."

The Jaspen Model Deepens and Expands

Although the pandemic has eased, the Jaspen Group continues to grow, now spread across five service regions. And its model has evolved over time, providing pre-employment services such as job-readiness and English as a second language (ESL) classes, as well as on-the-job support, such as industry-specific safety trainings. "We don't just drop somebody into a company and forget about them," says Duge. "We continue to work with them along with our employer partners—and that's how we help our business customers improve retention and manage turnover." Importantly, most of these workforce wraparound services are paid for primarily by employers.

Finally, in the face of mounting challenges for immigrant communities across the country, Jaspen has partnered with legal services and private attorneys to help both job applicants and their employers navigate the web of changing immigration laws and regulations now deeply impacting the Haitian community. And the Jaspen Group continues to play a leadership role in supporting the broader central Indiana Haitian community: Duge recently stepped down from his executive director position after four years with the Haitian Association of Indiana to lead a new project called the Kiskeya Complex in Lawrence, Indiana. When completed, the complex will provide the Haitian community with ESL programs; resources for housing, financial literacy, and social programs; and coworking spaces for small businesses in the nearby area.

The close coordination of the for-profit Jaspen Group and the nonprofit Haitian Association of Indiana has made a powerful impact on families throughout the Haitian community. And for Jaspen's employer customers, Duge underscores, "Our business clients have come to realize that to survive, they must go out and find a labor force very different from what they once hired. That's where we can help, because we are here. We are the community."

Retaining Your New Workers

Once you find a good source of untapped talent, you may also need help retaining your new workers, and their retention may benefit from targeted support services. Great workforce partners do not walk away once their clients are hired, but provide ongoing support through coaching, language interpretation, problem-solving, and troubleshooting—typically in close coordination with the client company and its HR team. Some workforce organizations, like JVS Boston (see case study, this chapter), provide tools and services to help with job redesign that can enhance job quality. Importantly, they do so in a way that builds your *own* internal capacity over time to attract and retain nontraditional candidates.

How Can You Find and Secure a Great Workforce Partner?

Like forging any other trusted vendor relationship, building a workforce partnership that taps nontraditional candidates will require work on your part, yet the payoff can be exceptionally valuable. You may begin with purely self-interested motivation, like filling your open positions, but you will likely end up with something much more profound: a partnership that not only improves your business but also strengthens your community. As Pete Strange of Messer Construction told us, "Selfish business decisions are a good place to start, then let the good feelings grow from success."[2]

The encouraging news is that many of the workforce organizations we describe ahead—or very similar ones—already operate in your community. The not-so-good news is that, like all vendors, their quality may vary greatly. To keep you from throwing your hands up in frustration, we also offer several tips for sorting the great from the not so great.

However, before we begin, we want to emphasize—as we have throughout this book—that you should start small and not reinvent the wheel. If you've already worked with a workforce organization and found the partnership fruitful, then, by all means, refine and expand it.

If you haven't previously engaged a workforce organization, then we recommend that you find a company in your community that's already known for its innovative workforce strategies—and ask its staff to recommend potential partners. When you begin vetting potential workforce partners, here are several things to keep in mind:

- *Work with an individual or individuals, not just the organization.* The key is finding a responsible individual within the workforce organization with whom you can engage closely to craft a genuine working relationship. You will be building a *long-term*, trusted, flexible, and adaptable partnership, so make sure that the individual you work with has those same personal and professional characteristics.
- *Be sure that your workforce partner has a customer-service culture.* You will certainly encounter potential workforce partners whose primary interest

is their own, idiosyncratic, closely held institutional rules and regulations. Avoid them. You can learn about an organization's culture most efficiently by interviewing their current or past customers and then interviewing your proposed point person. If your point person primarily asks questions about your challenges and speaks less about their services, then you're on the right track. If they claim that they can address and solve all your workforce challenges, don't buy it. You are looking for an organization that can underpromise and overdeliver. No single organization does everything well.

- *Be sure that you and your partner speak the same language.* If the organization uses lots of acronyms, exotic program titles, or regulatory language, be concerned. They should come prepared already understanding your company and industry—and if they don't, then they should at least be asking many good questions.
- *Check their track record.* You want a partner that is highly competent in finding and supporting untapped talent. If the organization claims to have that expertise, then it should be able to prove it with meaningful performance data—at the very least, rates of placement and length of retention. If they can't provide documented data, then move on.
- *Be patient and take the long view.* Some of the best workforce partnerships we've seen have lasted for decades, evolving as the labor market and business requirements demanded. As Ale' Mendoza, director of human resources at Optimax and long-time champion of workforce partnerships, has said, "Be vulnerable. Build relationships and trust. Build a community of common interests."[3]

Who Can Be a Great Workforce Partner?

As we've noted, you probably already work with a traditional employment organization, such as a staffing company. However, solving the forever-tight labor market and tapping untapped talent will require augmenting your traditional workforce sources with different types of organizations using quite different strategies. From the experiences of dozens of companies pursuing innovative workforce partnerships, as well as our own professional experience, we've identified five kinds of partners that we believe can help you find, and keep, nontraditional talent.

Community Colleges

Community colleges are perhaps the best-known workforce partners. There are more than one thousand community colleges located in practically every city and county across the United States. With nearly 40 percent of America's undergraduate students and more than 50 percent of students of color, community colleges enroll the nation's largest concentration of diverse workers who are seeking to increase their skills and improve their career opportunities. Community colleges are truly a home for untapped talent.[4]

Community colleges were once considered exclusively *educational* institutions—known primarily for offering an affordable way for students to transfer to a four-year college and secondarily for community members to acquire new knowledge and skills. Today, they are also becoming respected as *workforce-development* institutions, with extensive technical offerings and deep employer partnerships. Among the five workforce institutions we identify here, community colleges have the greatest scale, reach, resources, and physical and instructional capabilities, available to help employers fill vacancies and to help diverse students gain needed skills. To the extent that the US has a national workforce system, community colleges offer the main delivery mechanism.

That said, community colleges also face significant challenges, and therefore their value to employers ranges dramatically from impressive to frankly quite frustrating. One challenge, for example, is that community colleges are typically open enrollment institutions—meaning that they have no entrance exams or minimum grade-score requirements. Although this increases their accessibility, it can also result in exceptionally low completion rates, with many students never achieving any college-level certificate or degree in return for their hard-earned investment.

As noted previously, community colleges are also multipurpose institutions, and thus workforce development is typically just one of many priorities competing for attention and resources. As a result, community colleges can often be unreliable partners, with impenetrable bureaucracies, inflexible schedules, outdated curricula, and part-time, poorly paid faculty—all resulting in a limited willingness to approach your workforce challenges creatively.

Fortunately, many community colleges have learned how to overcome those challenges, offering highly valuable workforce resources. In 2023, Project on Workforce at Harvard[5] sought to understand the key elements that make a community college an outstanding workforce partner; in doing so, it identified a set of high performers that incorporate those elements.

Specifically, they identified the following five community colleges that have close partnerships with their regional employers, aligning their programs closely with regional labor market needs: Lorain County Community College, Ohio; Mississippi Gulf Coast Community College, Mississippi; Northern Virginia Community College, Virginia; Pima Community College, Arizona; and San Jacinto Community College, Texas.[6]

If you are fortunate enough to be located near one of these five colleges and aren't already partnering with them, you should be. Otherwise, you should get to know your own local community college and explore the possibilities of a creative workforce partnership with it. When you begin, consider these questions:

- *Is the college's leadership involved* in your region's area economic development organizations and business associations?
- *Does the college have an individual or individuals whose specific job is to partner with area employers?* Is that individual entrepreneurial, with a can-do attitude? Is their role a priority for the college, and is that role supported and well-resourced?
- *Does the college have programs that align with your region's key industries and skill requirements*, including, most importantly, your own?
- *Does the college have a track record* of attracting grant funding for programs that align with your region's key industries and skill requirements?
- *Does the college effectively support its students* and have a good track record in certificate and degree completion and postgraduation employment? Remarkably, very few community colleges track *employment* outcomes for their students—nor do most postsecondary institutions. That said, ask for whatever placement and retention employment outcome data they can provide.
- *Can the college provide you with recommendations from other regional employers*, attesting to successful employment partnerships?

If you like what you hear in answer to these questions, it will likely be well worth your time and effort to build such a partnership—but it will require a good deal of effort from you and your colleagues. And building a truly successful relationship will take time. Too many employers only engage with colleges at graduation; you can secure much better results if you structure an upstream relationship, by investing initially in low-cost activities, such as student visits to your workplace, and then later in more sophisticated activities, such as internships and other long-term, work-based learning initiatives.

Finally, community colleges often complain that their employer partners are not clear about what they need and are not willing to commit the time to build successful workforce programs. Fair or not, take the time to be very specific about what you require from the college—and at the same time, take the time to understand exactly what your college partner needs from you. The reward, in generating a steady source of high-quality, traditional and nontraditional candidates each year, will be substantial.

CASE STUDY: Optimax and Community Colleges—a Synergistic and Virtuous Cycle[7]

Optimax's[8] strategy to widen the hiring funnel led Ale' Mendoza, director of human resources, and his team to create exemplary partnerships with two higher education institutions in their Rochester-area region: Monroe Community College and Finger Lakes Community College.

According to Mendoza, "The community college infrastructure is very important to us. It's a continuation of our hiring and learning pipeline. We feel that it is very opportunistic for us to establish ourselves within these institutions as *partners*, because we have an obligation and a responsibility to continue to raise the threshold of our workforce. The concept of a plug-and-play technician or engineer is no longer realistic."

Optimax and other optics companies in its Rochester-area region are fortunate to benefit from an educational infrastructure that was built over many years with the support of legacy industry leaders like Kodak, Xerox, and Bausch & Lomb. Today, the region's postsecondary institutions make the greater Rochester area one of the only places in the world where a student can progress seamlessly in the field of optics technology: from a certificate to a two-year or four-year degree and all the way to a PhD.

Most recently, in 2022, Rochester was selected to be one of the technology hubs designated by the federal CHIPS Act. This means that the Rochester area is receiving a $100 billion investment that, among other elements, provides funding for a new Micron Technology semiconductor chip–manufacturing facility.

Optimax's experience with higher education partnerships leads Mendoza to offer five pieces of advice to companies that want to build or strengthen their community college partnerships:

- *Invite the leadership of your community college* to your organization to learn about what you do; that's the first step. It will help them understand your organization's business, technology, culture, challenges, and needs.
- *Employers must lead the charge*, but the community college leadership must be *receptive* to doing something a bit different—being open to taking the lead from the business partner to help design the curriculum, the program, and the delivery.
- *Commit dedicated resources to making the partnership happen*, even though that's always a challenge because everybody is so busy. Sometimes community colleges just don't understand what your company is about, and so they may naturally revert to the curriculum that they have in front of them or the guidelines outlined in a grant. Instead, industry must shape this with dedicated personnel who take the lead for the company.

  But it will not be cheap. Optimax, for example, has spent hundreds of thousands of dollars in dedicated staff time to ensure that these community college partnerships work well. Optimax personnel sit on the advisory committees and boards of multiple college programs that are important for their business. Also, Optimax personnel serve as adjunct faculty in several college optics programs.
- *Employers must know what they want*—but they must also be realistic about their expectations. Employers can't just say, "We want more candidates" or "We want people who will show up on time." That's not the community college's responsibility. The college's role is to be a *partner* to help create a learning pathway designed specifically to meet the key needs of the employer.
- *Employers must help community colleges be open to understanding what industry and academia can do together.* Is the college leadership

willing to experiment and learn? What kind of initiatives have they pursued to date? Do they want to truly partner with industry? What kinds of benefits would inspire and motivate them? What strategies do college leaders use to get out into their communities and stay informed about local needs and developments? Do they want to take chances and try out new models of education?

Two Exemplary Partnerships

Following these five maxims, Mendoza and his colleagues have developed deep and lasting partnerships with both Monroe Community College and Finger Lakes Community College.

Monroe Community College

Rochester's Monroe Community College[9] is Optimax's local two-year college. Monroe offers both certificate and associate degrees in optics, precision machining, and engineering science, with a well-articulated pathway to the four-year University of Rochester and the Rochester Institute of Technology. Optimax regularly recruits from these programs as a key element of its talent pipeline. Monroe has also built a *corporate college*, specifically designed to develop customized training for incumbent workers at Optimax and other companies in the region.

Importantly, these are not off-the-shelf classes. Personnel from Optimax work closely with Monroe staff to design curricula in real time to adapt to the rapidly changing technical needs of the industry. Depending on the equipment requirements and needs of the workers/students, courses are delivered on-site at Optimax, at the college or remotely, and they include foundational technical courses as well as leadership/management courses.

Finger Lakes Community College

Finger Lakes Community College,[10] located in nearby Canandaigua, New York, has developed a unique *clean room technology* program. That cutting-edge capacity is critically important for Optimax's semiconductor line of business, which has been a core part of the company's customer base since its inception. The semiconductor industry requires extremely high-precision optics, and part of the process of making precision optics for semiconductors is having the right clean room environment to inspect, clean, and package optics—which in turn requires specialized training.

Optimax is investing significant capital into its own new clean room, and it receives strong support and cutting-edge equipment from several key customers, who in return expect a high degree of exacting quality. To that end, Optimax and Finger Lakes jointly developed a unique, customized training program specifically tailored to their clean room operations. Because the technology is so new, Optimax and Finger Lakes could not depend on off-the-shelf courses, so they developed the program jointly over many months.

Reaching Earlier Within the Education System

Optimax also understands that its recruitment strategies need to start even earlier than college, so the company works closely with area high schools to grow interest in the optics field and recruit eventual employees. Many Rochester-area high schools now offer dual-enrollment courses that directly tie into the optics program at the regional colleges.

Optimax also works closely with area vocational-technical high schools, providing career exploration opportunities such as co-ops and job shadowing, instructors, plant visits, and classroom presentations—and when they find great candidates, they hire them. If workers want to continue their education with college-level classes, Optimax will hire them on a part-time basis and pay for all of their further education.

A Virtuous Cycle

Optimax has created a virtuous cycle with its community college partnerships—sharing knowledge, resources, grants, and even personnel back and forth among the institutions—in turn strengthening the regional optics industry, the local educational infrastructure, and the entire community.

Mendoza stresses, "There's a lifelong learning element required at least within advanced manufacturing environments. Employers must support the continuing education pathways that their employees are on. And the better the company can do that, the better the employees become at their jobs, which makes them even more important to the business—which in turn makes the business even more successful."

Career and Technical Education High Schools

In some industries, such as manufacturing, construction, automotive, and food service, vocational-technical high schools can be an excellent workforce development partner of choice. More than eight million high school students are enrolled in career and technical education (CTE) programs nationwide, and that number is steadily growing.

Unfortunately, many districts still maintain old-school voc-tech programs that are hobbled by questionable academic rigor and low graduation rates. However, in recent years, some exemplary districts have incorporated high academic standards that feature hands-on vocational training, thereby effectively supporting students who choose to go directly into the workforce or on to two- or four-year colleges. In some communities, partnerships between CTE high schools, community colleges, and employers have together launched *career pathway* programs that enable students to gain advanced technical skills that are in high demand in their region.

In many districts, CTE programs have long-standing partnerships with area employers, often hiring company employees as instructors and incorporating student internships into their hiring strategies. Optimax in Ontario, New York, is in regular touch with its local CTE high school faculty to promote career opportunities and shape curricula and programming.

Messer Construction[11] of Cincinnati, Ohio, is deeply committed to building diverse talent pipelines for its own and its suppliers' workforces and therefore strongly encourages its personnel to engage directly with area schools, working closely with teachers, sharing opportunities with students, and developing externships at the company. Messer also partners with Charlotte Mecklenburg Schools and the nonprofit Goodwill Industries to operate the Partnership for Inclusive Employment and Careers Excellence (PIECE),[12] which provides CTE training programs in construction and renewable energy.

Industries with jobs that require only a high school diploma still dominate CTE partnerships. However, in recent years, CTE high schools in some districts have begun to focus on newer, expanding industries in their districts.

For example, P-TECH[13] is a science, technology, engineering, and mathematics (STEM) CTE high school in Brooklyn, New York. P-TECH partners closely with IBM, which recently hired nearly half of P-TECH's first year's graduates. P-TECH's two Brooklyn-based programs, computer systems technology and electromechanical engineering technology, are closely aligned with IBM's hiring needs. P-TECH also hosts a national network of close to three hundred CTE high schools across the country, offering programs in a range of growing industries within extensive industry partnerships.[14]

Community-Based Workforce Intermediaries

The term *community-based workforce intermediary* describes a wide range of workforce organizations—typically, though not exclusively, nonprofits—that act as brokers between workers and employers. They often play an influential role in regional labor markets, working with employer associations, philanthropies, and governments in shaping workforce strategies and public policies.

At their best, they identify business and worker needs; design and implement innovative recruitment, training, and retention strategies; find and aggregate funding sources; and broker or directly deliver workforce services. A series of papers published in 2019 by the Boston Foundation[15] described four key features of high-performing, or *next-gen*, workforce intermediaries. They are market-responsive with a strong customer service culture; focused not on just any job but on engaging to *improve* job quality; deeply embedded in and valued by their regional employers and employer organizations; and able to provide quality services at a large scale, including efforts to improve public and private workforce systems.

CASE STUDY: Jewish Vocational Service[16]

Jewish Vocational Service (JVS)[17] is a Boston-based workforce intermediary founded in 1938 by the Jewish community to assist Jewish refugees from Europe—as well as Jewish workers already in the Boston area who were facing antisemitic workplace discrimination—in learning English, attaining vocational skills, and finding jobs.

Today, JVS Boston is the largest workforce development organization serving the Boston region, and one of the largest in the country. JVS provides skills training, coaching, and job-placement services annually to more than ten thousand individuals, many of them English language learners. At the same time, JVS provides training, placement, and job redesign services to more than one hundred local companies. JVS is a nonprofit company, valued by regional employers for its deep customer service culture, ability to innovate to meet its client and customer needs, and proven capacity to respond rapidly to changes in the region's business and labor markets.

JVS's Employer Partnerships

JVS is well known for its deep and long-standing employer partnerships, some of which are nearly thirty years old. In the early 2000s, JVS made a strategic decision to develop a highly sophisticated employer engagement strategy, modeled on the client-relationship management tactics used by the for-profit staffing industry. Core to the JVS employer engagement model are three components:

- *A deep understanding of the employer* and what "keeps them up at night"
- *A customer-service delivery model* that constantly underpromises and overdelivers
- *An indispensable concentration* on solving their clients' staffing and training needs

To deliver this employer engagement model, JVS hires and trains staff to maintain a balance of skills necessary to engage simultaneously with both employers, as JVS's customers, and job seekers, as JVS's mission-driven constituents.

JVS's Employer Engagement Strategy

In the late 1990s, many companies—particularly, though not exclusively, based in the health-care industry—began contracting with JVS to provide on-site English and skills training for their employees. By

2021, these contracts grew into a multi-million-dollar service line for JVS, with dozens of companies and hundreds of workers receiving on-site and remote English, computer, and specialized skills training courses provided by JVS instructors.

JVS President and CEO Kira Khazatsky, herself an immigrant to Boston from the former Soviet Union, has been with the organization for nearly twenty years. She started as an English for speakers of other languages (ESOL) volunteer teacher, eventually climbing JVS's career ladder to take the helm of the organization in 2022. According to Khazatsky, "What makes JVS so valuable to our employer partners is our ability to embed ourselves in the organization we are serving. We essentially become an extension of their recruiting and workforce development capacity. Typically, employers would prefer not to become adult education providers themselves—yet they need their employees to have those skills. This creates a mutually beneficial opportunity in which the employer is able to offer high-quality training through JVS, and JVS is able to impact thousands of job seekers who are the core of our mission."

Customized Recruitment and Training

For many years, JVS offered a growing number of industry- and occupation-specific training programs for job seekers. Through JVS's hiring and retention process, these programs provided both in-person and remote specialized skills training, as well as intensive coaching and student support.

Then, as the Boston-area labor market tightened over the last decade, employers began looking to JVS to help them find, prepare, and support untapped talent. Through its extensive roots within local communities and community organizations, JVS often has a deeper understanding of regional talent pools than their employer partners. At the same time, JVS staff spend a great deal of time helping job seekers make informed and realistic decisions about industries, job opportunities, and what would make a great fit for each individual. JVS's comprehensive coaching model also follows the job seeker into and through a new job placement, and even thereafter, continuing to support the individual along his or her professional growth pathways.

Most recently, JVS has developed a new training model known as the Talent Pipeline in partnership with several major local employers. Through this model, employers identify open positions in key, hard-to-fill areas. JVS in turn recruits and screens applicants accordingly. With employer approval, the trainees are then "pre-hired" and trained at both the JVS training site and their new employer's worksite—and in many cases, participants are paid during training. After completion of their training, the new workers begin full-time employment.

The key to the success of this program is the close partnership that JVS develops with each employer, with JVS staff investing many hours into learning about the industry, relevant job requirements, and all the unique elements that make for a successful employee fit with each specific employer.

In designing the Talent Pipeline model, JVS leveraged the tight labor market to flip the traditional workforce development model on its head: Rather than train individuals for a job they simply hoped to get, JVS created predictability for both the employer and the job seeker. According to Khazatsky, "The Talent Pipeline model offers a customized set of training and support services designed to address the gap between the skills that employers are seeking and those that job seekers are looking to gain. JVS's deep understanding of both employer and job seeker positions the agency to play a critical intermediary role."

JVS's Job Quality Benchmarking Index

In 2018, with the job market continuing to tighten, JVS made a strategic shift—moving away from the traditional view in workforce development that "any job is better than no job," and focusing instead on the *quality* of the jobs offered by JVS's employer partners. After spending more than six months polling both its clients and staff, and doing extensive field research, JVS learned more clearly that the definition of *job quality* was different for different workers. In response,

JVS developed a flexible, five-part framework for job quality, one that measures wages, benefits, scheduling, career opportunities, and supportive work environments.

This five-part framework was then converted into an online employer self-survey, with detailed questions in each of the five categories. After taking the survey to measure the job quality of specific positions within their company, the user receives a report that compares their own company's job quality measurements to comparable positions at similar companies within the region's labor market.

Thanks to the tool now known as the Job Quality Benchmarking Index (JQBI),[18] JVS has issued more than three hundred reports to Boston-region companies, providing valuable insights into their job quality status versus that of their competitors, as well as practical suggestions for how to improve their job quality standing. JVS also uses the data from the JQBI to advise workforce participants on the best job openings to pursue given their personal job quality priorities. As a result, nearly 50 percent of JVS's job-seeking clients are now employed in quality jobs, up from 10 percent when the JQBI project started.

At the national level, the National Fund for Workforce Solutions is one organization that supports local and regional "donor collaboratives" in order to expressly encourage and strengthen community-based workforce intermediaries.[19] Founded in 2007 by a group of major national philanthropies—including the Ford, Annie E. Casey, Hitachi, and Harry and Jeanette Weinberg Foundations—the fund now supports the work of more than thirty regional workforce funder collaboratives across the country. The fund is the nation's leading workforce entity, providing grant funding, supporting innovation, and helping to evaluate effective workforce intermediaries.

Most major cities have one or more workforce intermediaries affiliated with the National Fund for Workforce Solutions. For example, the Chicagoland Workforce Funder Alliance supports several local intermediaries in Chicago,[20] including Cara Plus, a nonprofit that specializes in business partnerships to tap the untapped talent of individuals with a criminal record.[21] Civic Works[22] in Baltimore provides training for the energy conservation industry, leveraging the economic power of government procurement to help tap Baltimore's untapped talent. And JVS[23] of San Francisco provides extensive recruitment, training, IT support, and employer-retention services in the health care, biotech, financial, and other key industries.

If you are seeking an effective workforce partner in your area, researching the collaborative networks of the National Fund for Workforce Solutions is a good place to start. The employer partnerships the organization has helped encourage are deep and effective, with some in operation for more than twenty-five years.

Finally, some community-based workforce partners focus within a specific industry, deploying what is called a "sectoral workforce strategy." For example, within the long-term care industry, the leading sectoral workforce partner is PHI, based in New York City.[24] For more than thirty-five years, PHI has consulted across more than thirty states to a range of home care and residential care providers.

PHI works to improve the quality of care for those who are elderly or living with a disability by improving the quality of the job of the direct care worker. The organization is particularly known for its "coaching approach" to supervisory training, peer mentor training, and entry-level training services, as well as its policy advisory services to many state governmental workforce and healthcare agencies. PHI is also the nonprofit affiliate of Cooperative Home Care Associates, the largest worker cooperative in the US (see case studies in chapters 2 and 3).

Another exemplary sectoral workforce organization is Per Scholas, which focuses explicitly within the tech industry.

CASE STUDY: Per Scholas—the Business Logic of Partnering[25]

Per Scholas[26] is a nonprofit workforce development intermediary founded in the Bronx borough of New York in 1995 to train low-income and racially diverse adults to repair computers. As the technology industry changed, Per Scholas changed as well, focusing on recruiting, training, and supporting untapped talent for the technology industry.

Three accomplishments place Per Scholas at the head of the pack of workforce intermediaries. First, it is one of the few such organizations that has successfully replicated its model, now training five thousand people annually across twenty-four cities, including New York, Los Angeles, Boston, Chicago, Pittsburgh, Phoenix, and Dallas. Second, it is one of only a handful of workforce intermediaries that has proven the effectiveness of its model through two gold standard random control studies—both of which documented statistically significant positive employment and earnings outcomes for Per Scholas clients.

And third, Per Scholas has developed strong, direct relationships with both national technology companies and regional companies seeking talent within its twenty-four urban markets. Per Scholas now develops talent pipelines for companies such as TEKsystems, Guardian Life Insurance, and Wells Fargo, with more than half the cost of its services paid directly by the employers.

Evolution of the Per Scholas Model

Beginning in the late 1990s, Per Scholas began offering training for *A+ certification*, an entry-level credential widely recognized as a qualification for technical support and IT operations. The organization has continued to adapt to changing technology industry training needs by adding other forms of training and certification, such as for networking, cybersecurity, desktop support, software development, and cloud support.

Over time, Per Scholas expanded its training program length from twelve to fifteen weeks. Founder and CEO Plineo Ayala describes the organization's changes: "It's been an amazing journey with many challenges over the last several years—like COVID-19 and inflation—but we're in a great place and thinking hard about the next wave of growth."

In addition to IT training, Per Scholas now helps place its graduates in IT businesses by providing them with career-readiness services and developing strong employer pipeline relationships. Per Scholas also provides ongoing alumni services for its graduates, including upskilling opportunities.

Changing the Pitch

Although technology hiring has somewhat paused in recent years—due to economic uncertainties, the unknown impact of AI, and retrenchment of the tech industry after rapid growth—Per Scholas maintains a strong placement track record for its graduates. In its early years, Per Scholas's pitch to employers emphasized its ability to help companies diversify their talent pool. For example, Per Scholas participants are significantly more racially and ethnically diverse than typical new hires in the same industries and locations: 87 percent are people of color, and 79 percent belong to minorities that are underrepresented in IT jobs.

However, as the labor market continued to tighten, Per Scholas's appeal to the economic self-interest of its business partners began to prevail, and those arguments are strong. Ayala maintains that "Per Scholas's value added beyond racial diversity is that we can reduce companies' recruitment and turnover costs. We tell our employer customers that it's an economic imperative for you, right? If you really think about this talent pool we're creating for you, it's saving you money."

And Per Scholas's outcome data confirm his pitch: The organization's hires have substantially lower turnover rates than other newly hired workers in the same industries and location. When combined with savings from obviating the need for other costly recruitment alternatives, employers can see savings of up to $1,800 per employee annually.[27]

Refining the Model

As Per Scholas has expanded, it has continued to adapt and adjust to rapidly changing industry talent requirements. As Ayala notes, "In the coming years, a software engineer is going to be a very different kind of job. I do think AI is a bit overblown and that the net job loss will be minimal. However, I do think that the entry-level requirements are going to go up; that participants are going to need more training to get into these jobs." In response, Per Scholas is considering extending its program as it adds more skills training into its curricula while, at the same time, working tirelessly to keep up with rapidly changing company-partnership demands.

Refinements to the Per Scholas model are not limited to training curricula. For the many students whose math and English skills are not yet sufficient to succeed in Per Scholas's skill-based classes, the organization now partners with many other agencies to create bridges to Per Scholas's programs. In addition, Per Scholas has expanded its student-support services, including creating a loan program for students to help manage emergencies or other financial demands during their training period.

A Proven Tech Partner

With its proven model, commitment to continuous improvement, wide geographic reach, and customer service ethos, Per Scholas is an outstanding workforce partner for companies looking to fill and diversify their technology talent requirements in a rapidly changing environment. According to Ayala:

> Companies struggle to find talent and are often just fighting each other for college graduates. Some of them are beginning to upskill their entry-level workers, to fill these new roles with a new definition of *entry level*, which is much more sophisticated than what they had before.
>
> And so, what our business clients are saying to us is, "Well, we haven't been able to solve how we backfill internally, so we're going to need some pool of entry-level people to train to get into that second tier." And I think therein lies the opportunity to create a different role, with a different set of skills—to be a pipeline that companies can upscale to those jobs. That's what we're trying to figure out.

Given its now documented track record of success, innovation, and adaptation, Per Scholas will indeed figure that out.

Organized Labor: Training and Education Affiliates

Some of you may have a long-standing relationship with a union that represents your workforce. For others, perhaps labor unions are to be avoided at all costs.

Whatever your direct experience, unions are an important voice of American workers and can offer valuable resources for addressing the forever-tight labor market. It is important to note that, after decades of shrinkage, the American union movement has some wind in its sails: Many years of real earnings declines and job quality erosion have boosted worker interest in joining a union to its highest level since 1965.[28] General US popular support for unionization now stands at 70 percent.[29]

For the first two-thirds of the twentieth century, labor unions were a central element of US economic success. They contributed not only to their members' growing wages, benefits, and overall prosperity, but also to employer success in product innovation, operations, benefit systems, job quality, and a highly trained workforce.[30]

Granted, union membership continues to be low, particularly in the private sector, but growing numbers of union drives and growing interest in union affiliation by workers have led some business leaders to consider a less hostile position—and, in some cases, even to fully embrace what unions can contribute to their operations.

For example, technology giant Microsoft and retailer IKEA have publicly committed to not oppose efforts by their employees to unionize. Kaiser Permanente, the California-based health care giant, is investing deeply in its union relationship, with over four thousand unit-based teams designed to jointly problem-solve, improve productivity, and ultimately increase profitability.

For our purposes here, we want to emphasize that US unions have a long history of training and preparing workers for success in the workplace. For example, in many major American cities, such as New York, Boston, and San Francisco, union apprenticeship programs are the primary source of high-quality, paid training for the building trades. Major contractors and workers alike depend upon these programs to ensure good jobs, safety, and quality construction. And, importantly, apprentices typically are paid while they learn their trades.

A legitimate criticism of union apprenticeship programs in the building trades, and construction employment in general, for that matter, is that too little untapped talent—women and individuals of color in particular—have been able to participate. Fortunately, in recent years, many preapprenticeship programs have been launched to reach into more diverse communities. *Preapprenticeships* prepare individuals with the foundational skills, knowledge, and experience needed to succeed in the more formal *registered apprenticeship* training programs, which in turn lead directly to employment within the trades.

One outstanding preapprenticeship program in Rhode Island, Building Futures,[31] prepares hundreds of workers and young adults, primarily of color, to enter and successfully complete union apprenticeship programs. Building Futures operates preapprenticeship programs in all the major trades and maintains deep relationships with both craft unions and major construction companies throughout Rhode Island.

Beyond the building trades apprenticeships, several unions operate large-scale training centers in partnership with their employer partners. For example, UNITE HERE, a union that represents hotel, culinary, and other hospitality workers, operates a renowned culinary and hospitality training facility in Las Vegas.[32] And Boston Education, Skills & Training (BEST)[33] (see the following case study) operates a training center for the region's hospitality industry, providing hospitality and culinary training for individuals seeking to enter the industry, as well as for incumbent workers within participating unionized hotels and casinos.

CASE STUDY: BEST Labor-Management Partnership[34]

When the COVID-19 pandemic swept through the country, Boston's vibrant hospitality industry shut down overnight, thrusting thousands of workers into immediate financial crisis. Today, the industry has come roaring back, and at the center of its revival are the combined efforts of UNITE HERE Local 26,[35] the union that represents nearly three-quarters of the region's hospitality workers, and UNITE's training arm, BEST.

BEST, a Boston nonprofit, was founded in 2004 under a Taft-Hartley labor-management agreement between the unionized hotel properties and the hotel workers' union. BEST helps workers in unionized hotels increase their skills, gain certifications to perform their jobs more effectively, and, if they choose to do so, build a career within the industry. These benefits are offered at no cost to the workers, paid for by a fourteen-cents-per-hour-worked contribution provided by each unionized employer. BEST also prepares candidates who want to enter the hospitality industry through skills training and career coaching, primarily in housekeeping and culinary areas—the two largest classifications in a hotel—funded through a combination of public, philanthropic, and private sources.

Recovering from the Pandemic

According to BEST's executive director, Aisha Necoechea, the hospitality industry has substantially recovered from COVID-19, though it has taken several years and much struggle. As the pandemic receded, and hotels were refilling with tourists and business travelers, workers were difficult to find; hotels had lost many of their former employees, who had either retired or moved to other employment.

In response to the dearth of available workers, hotels leaned heavily on those who remained by substantially increasing overtime assignments. By late 2023, however, BEST saw a major uptick in the interest level among job seekers looking to enter the industry, and their classes began to refill—largely with new immigrant arrivals. Yet hotels continued to rely on overtime rather than stepping up new hires, a practice that became a major item of contention in contract negotiations.

According to Necoechea, "The hotels could not keep up with the amount of business and the amount of required work hours with the limited number of employees they had. They were not hiring fast enough so that workers could return to regular hours. In some ways workers appreciate it because they can earn more in overtime, but if that becomes your new status quo, and you work sixty or seventy hours a week, it's not sustainable for either the workers or the hotels."

Navigating Online Job Application Systems

BEST has taken several steps to help the hotels fill open positions. One of the major barriers for new hires is that nearly all hotels moved to online hiring systems during the pandemic—and they continue to rely on these systems today. In response, BEST now works closely with its students, most of whom are English language learners, to navigate through the complex, online job application systems that otherwise too often screen out their students. This helps applicants connect more quickly and easily to each hotel's hiring managers.

Also, BEST is currently developing a *centralized job board* that will host all unionized hotel jobs within a single portal, lowering the barrier of job applicants needing to navigate multiple hotel portals to find available positions. In the latest round of contract negotiations, the hotel workers' union included hiring language that prioritizes BEST referrals into available jobs.

BEST is also helping area hotels fill positions by upskilling incumbent workers. According to Necoechea, hotels have recently begun taking greater advantage of BEST's incumbent worker training that the hotels are already paying for in order to develop the talent they already have. Necoechea explains:

> For years, hotels have indicated that finding cooks is one of their biggest challenges. They need something more than someone who has cooked at McDonald's, and graduates of schools like the Culinary Institute of America are hard to come by. Where's the happy medium? So we developed a culinary training program where we train both job seekers and incumbent workers who have kitchen work experience and want to move into better jobs.
>
> For incumbent workers, a chef can identify a steward who is good in the kitchen, understands the basics, and is often pulled in to do prep jobs. They recommend them, and the workers can then take the culinary training program and potentially move into a line-cook position. The steward position, which is easier to fill, then becomes open, and a new job seeker enters the industry. The training takes place in one of the unionized professional hotel kitchens, and the hard-skills trainers are also executive chefs from partner hotels. That way, we've developed the curriculum knowing what the hotels need.

Over the last two years, BEST has moved into providing on-site—during paid work time—industry-recognized certification classes, including CPR/AED, MA Allergens, ServSafe Food Safety, and TIPS. Classes are free for union members through their contracted education benefits. If hotels request it, BEST also provides, on a fee-for-service basis, slots within these same classes to nonunion members, and at times even to hotel/restaurant managers.

The hotel workers' union's advocacy for workers—combined with BEST's skills training, career coaching, placement, and upskilling support—contributes to unionized hotel workers accessing high-quality jobs. Under the union's new contract, by 2028, the union rate for housekeepers will be $38.80/hour, or over $80,000/year for a full-time position, which is a $10/hour increase over the current hourly rate of $28.80.

The current benefit contribution has an additional value of $10.65 per hour worked, and that is also likely to increase in the new contract. Benefits include a full wellness plan—health, dental, vision, prescription coverage, and employee assistance; pension benefits; a legal assistance plan; a first-time home-buyer loan; and, of course, access to BEST's training and education classes.

Despite contentious contract negotiations, many hotel managers and hiring managers understand and appreciate the great value BEST provides in training, hiring, and upskilling their employees. According to Jon Cresslin, managing director of the Hilton Boston Park Plaza hotel,

> BEST has been an incredibly valuable partner to the Hilton Boston Park Plaza for many years. We are and shall remain supportive and collaborative by offering job shadowing and supporting other key areas of their programs. Recently, we hired nine of the graduates of the job-seeker program and we are ready to hire five from the cohort in session. We are delighted to have been actively involved in their inaugural culinary training program—a testament to how BEST hears the employer needs and actions with thoughtfulness, flexibility, and nimbleness."[36]

Within other industries, several health care unions also have long-established, deeply respected Taft-Hartley-based training and education affiliates. For example, in 1974 the National Union of Hospital and Health Care Employees (NUHHCE) joined with eleven Philadelphia-area hospitals to establish the District 1199C Training and Upgrading Fund.[37] The fund now trains more than four thousand health care workers annually in its thirty-five-thousand-square-foot Breslin Learning Center. The fund's programming helps fill vacancies with newly trained workers and provides education and skills upgrading for incumbent workers to upgrade into higher-level positions.

Similarly, in New York, Massachusetts, California, Washington State, and many other regions, the Service Employees International Union (SEIU) cosponsors with employers the largest network of health care worker training and upgrading programs in the nation.[38]

Public Workforce Agencies

Although community colleges are the largest public source of workforce partnerships, the publicly funded workforce-development system, supported by the federal Workforce Innovation and Opportunity Act (WIOA), also provides resources that can help you compete within the forever-tight labor market—though there is evidence that these resources may be significantly reduced in future federal budgets. In particular, two components of the WIOA system that we'll discuss next may prove helpful.

Workforce Investment Boards Every region of every state in the country has a Workforce Investment Board (WIB), typically organized by state or local government to develop regional workforce strategies. The WIBs also distribute federal, and sometimes state, funding to support those strategies. These boards, which include business, civic, union, community, and political leaders, are empowered to act as a strategic workforce planning hub for the regional or state economy.

In truth, WIB performance is a very mixed bag. Some WIBs have dynamic and entrepreneurial boards that truly lead and guide workforce development in their region, while others seem to merely check the bureaucratic boxes. At their best, WIBs are industry led—in fact, by law, WIBs must be chaired by an employer—and can be deeply participatory and entrepreneurial.

There are many examples of very effective WIBs that have developed innovative programming specifically designed to address the needs of both their region's growing industries and their skilled workforces. The best become expert in finding and securing both private and public funds and engage in continuous improvement to ensure that they remain up-to-date given constant changes in industry and labor-market demands.[39]

If you are fortunate enough to have such a WIB in your community, consider joining it; they are often looking for entrepreneurial business leadership. Many business leaders who we have interviewed have found that their local WIB has provided them with resources, connections, and ideas for improving their own company's workforce development strategies.

One-Stop Career Centers WIBs also fund and oversee American Job Centers (often called *one-stop career centers*) in cities and regions of every state. These centers were designed to help unemployed individuals access training and connect to jobs.

Like WIBs, one-stop career centers have quite a mixed record. In many cases, the centers act simply as unemployment insurance compliance monitors, places where individuals collecting public unemployment benefits are required to demonstrate that they are seeking employment in good faith. Yet in the best of cases, the centers play an important role in connecting untapped talent to participating employers through job fairs, individual referrals, and, in some cases, sophisticated applicant screening and preparation.

Other Public Workforce Services In addition to the WIOA-funded services, there exist federal workforce funding sources from the US Department of Labor, the US Department of Commerce, and many other federal agencies, though many have recently experienced contract rescissions and budget reductions. Both the Department of Labor and the Department of Commerce regularly offer workforce funding targeted for specific industries, occupations, or workers. Some of these funding streams can provide millions of dollars for customized, employer-led workforce programming.

Also, if you are a manufacturer, then you may want to connect to the Manufacturing Extension Partnership (MEP) in your region.[40] These regional organizations were created by the National Institute of Standards and Technology (NIST) to help manufacturers increase their competitiveness, including upgrading the skills of their workforce.

Finally, many state and city governments offer workforce funding, some of which is specifically designed to build an employer's talent-development capacity. In addition, more than twenty states direct a small portion of their unemployment insurance tax revenue to provide grants for companies to train their incumbent workers.

If you are lucky enough to have an effective WIB in your backyard, you can rely on it to identify and apply for these various types of resources. If your company is large enough to have its own government relations staff or consultant, they should be asked to alert you to these opportunities and help guide you through each process.

That Was a Lot of Information . . .

Perhaps too much? Yet the many companies we have worked with over the years, and the many employers we have interviewed for this book, have convinced us that you can and should find great workforce partners to help you address the forever-tight job market. Simply stated, you don't have to confront your workforce challenges alone.

And, as always: Start small, be patient, and celebrate your wins.

Conclusion

We are very aware that you may be feeling a bit challenged upon finishing this book, both by the prospect of managing in a forever-tight labor market and by the number and range of possible solutions we've offered. However, we hope that the many practices and case examples we have offered—from companies of widely varying sizes, industries, and geographies—will reassure you that there are practical and effective solutions to your specific hiring challenges.

Most importantly, we hope that you, like us, find these case examples inspirational, demonstrating the creativity and tenacity of American employers in the face of a very challenging labor-market environment. Yours is a once-in-a-generation opportunity to redefine what it means to be a *savvy employer* within the new economic reality of a forever-tight labor market.

The Three Principles

We have (mostly) resisted the temptation to prescribe exactly how to succeed in a forever-tight labor market. Still, there are three principles that we hope you carry with you as you travel on this journey.

First, resist the temptation to just wait for the economic weather to change, even if many of your peers decide instead to follow the "path of least persistence." Although we can't predict it with 100 percent certainty, the data strongly indicate that the economic *climate* forecasts a forever-tight labor market. So if you've already begun your business-focused workforce journey, keep it going, and growing—and if you haven't, it's clearly time to get started.

Second, as we've demonstrated throughout the book, prioritize people: Talk to your employees (often), *listen* to what they're saying (always), and act on their best insights as much and as quickly as you can.

. . . Even in the Navy

In his classic management book *It's Your Ship: Management Techniques from the Best Damn Ship in the Navy*,[1] former Navy Commander Michael Abrashoff chronicled his captaining of more than three hundred sailors on the guided-missile destroyer *USS Benfold*. Throughout the book, Abrashoff dramatizes his quite un-Navy-like management style of actually *listening* to his sailors—rather than simply giving traditional top-down orders.

Abrashoff recounts one memorable instance early in his command when one young sailor informed him that currently the entire 505-foot ship was sanded down and repainted *six times* each year. "The sailor suggested a better way: Use stainless steel bolts and nuts to replace the ferrous-metal ones that streaked rust down the sides of the ship."[2] The result: the ship required repainting just once annually, with tens of thousands of hours saved, not to mention a significant boost in ship morale.

Third, take things one small step at a time, celebrate your wins, and build on your successes. Your organization's systems, structures, and cultures weren't built overnight—so they won't change easily, despite your every effort and intent.

And should you need one final word of encouragement, our dear colleague and nationally recognized training specialist Peggy Powell has always reminded us: "The map is not the journey."[3] Facing resistance head-on—acknowledging honestly what is truly at play and then responding to that resistance creatively—can be an exciting process that may well appeal to your entrepreneurial, problem-solving spirit.

The journey is always far more interesting than the map.

Acknowledgments

This book is the result of hours of conversation with colleagues, mentors, friends, family, and of course each other. First and foremost, we are especially grateful to the many individuals who were so willing to share their stories with us and help us turn those case studies into valuable lessons for others. We hope that we have faithfully captured the essence of these stories and shared successfully what we found so inspiring about each one of them.

We also want to thank our former colleagues at JVS Boston (now led by President and CEO Kira Khazatsky) and at PHI (now led by President and CEO Jodi Sturgeon) for helping to shape our professional values and worldviews through many years of successes, challenges, and continuous learning. Both continue to demonstrate innovative ways for workers and employers to fully tap talent, capabilities, and opportunity.

Importantly, Eastern Bank and the Eastern Bank Foundation have supported this project from its inception, and we want to thank the bank's CEO, Bob Rivers, and the former president of its foundation, Nancy Stager, for living the values expressed in this book and providing inspiration and key resources to make its publication possible.

We also wish to thank Catherine Woods, executive editor, economics, business, and finance at the MIT Press: From our very first discussions, she has been exceptionally supportive, encouraging, and thoughtful in guiding this book to publication.

Also, our two remarkable research assistants from the Harvard Kennedy School of Government and Project on Workforce at Harvard, Mehr Pasricha and Aashi Agarwal, were always willing to dig up and interpret important data and sometimes elusive case examples. Their editing and writing skills were unequaled and led to the inclusion of their exceptional Market Basket case study.

Several good friends who are also intellectual leaders in their fields provided important insights and referrals and were willing to read and edit many drafts. Economists Paul Osterman, Barry Bluestone, and Dorie Seavey, as well as long-time workforce development leader Fred Dedrick, showed great generosity of spirit and insight throughout the process.

Finally, we want to thank our families, who provided moral support, of course, but also fair and honest feedback and great suggestions for issues and case examples to pursue in our research. James Steinberg created the beautiful cover art. In particular, our spouses (Carol Steinberg and Peg Dawson—both excellent, widely published writers themselves) lovingly supported the time we spent buried in this project, tolerated our whingeing, and celebrated our accomplishments along the way.

Notes

Introduction

1. "BLS Data Viewer," US Bureau of Labor Statistics, accessed September 30, 2025, https://www.bls.gov/charts/employment-situation/civilian-unemployment-rate.htm.

2. "Employment Level—Native Born (LNU02073413)," Federal Reserve Bank of St. Louis, accessed May 2, 2025, https://fred.stlouisfed.org/series/LNU02073413.

3. Joseph Wallace, "Five Commonly Misattributed Quotations," *MLA Style Center*, December 15, 2021, https://style.mla.org/five-commonly-misattributed-quotations/.

4. Richard Beckhard and Reuben T. Harris, *Organizational Transitions: Understanding Complex Change* (Addison-Wesley, 1977).

5. Ale' Mendoza, director of human resources at Optimax, interview with the authors, October 8, 2024.

6. See https://www.optimaxsi.com/.

7. US Department of Commerce, *Job Quality Toolkit* (US Department of Commerce, August 2022), https://cdn-jobquality.results4america.org/content/uploads/Job-Quality-Toolkit.pdf.

Chapter 1

1. "Labor Force Statistics from the Current Population Survey," US Bureau of Labor Statistics, accessed September 30, 2025, https://www.bls.gov/cps/.

2. Ron Hetrick, Hannah Grieser, and Tim Hatton, *The Rising Storm* (Lightcast, 2024), 3, https://lightcast.io/resources/research/the-rising-storm.

3. US Census Bureau, "U.S. Population Projected to Begin Declining in Second Half of Century," press release, November 9, 2023, https://www.census.gov/newsroom/press-releases/2023/population-projections.html.

4. Congressional Budget Office, *The Demographic Outlook: 2024 to 2054* (Congressional Budget Office, January 2024), https://www.cbo.gov/publication/59899.

5. "UN Projects World Population to Peak Within This Century," United Nations, Department of Economic and Social Affairs, July 11, 2024, https://www.un.org/en/UN-projects-world-population-to-peak-within-this-century#:~:text=1.

6. "Civilian Labor Force Participation Rate," US Bureau of Labor Statistics, accessed September 29, 2025, https://www.bls.gov/charts/employment-situation/civilian-labor-force-participation-rate.htm; and US Bureau of Labor Statistics, "Employment Projections," accessed September 29, 2025, https://www.bls.gov/emp/tables/civilian-labor-force-participation-rate.htm.

7. Justin Lahart, "The Jobs Numbers Aren't Adding Up. Immigration Helps Explain Why," *Wall Street Journal*, April 3, 2024, https://www.wsj.com/economy/jobs/unemployment-jobs-report-us-immigration-surge-8e260f47?utm_source.

8. David Leonhardt, "Recent Immigration Surge Has Been Largest in U.S. History," *New York Times*, December 11, 2024, https://www.nytimes.com/2024/12/11/briefing/us-immigration-surge.html.

9. "Employment Level—Native Born (LNU02073413)," Federal Reserve Bank of St. Louis, accessed May 2, 2025, https://fred.stlouisfed.org/series/LNU02073413.

10. "Employment Level—Native Born."

11. Paul Kiernan, "How Immigration Remade the U.S. Labor Force," *Wall Street Journal*, September 4, 2024, https://www.wsj.com/economy/how-immigration-remade-the-u-s-labor-force-716c18ee.

12. Leonhardt, "Recent Immigration Surge."

13. Kiernan, "Immigration Remade U.S. Labor Force."

14. Stephanie Kramer and Jeffrey S. Passel, "What the Data Say About Immigrants in the U.S.," Pew Research Center, August 21, 2025.

15. Beatrice Nolan, "Anthropic Researchers Predict a 'Pretty Terrible Decade' for Humans as AI Could Wipe Out White Collar Jobs," *Fortune*, June 5, 2025, https://fortune.com/2025/06/05/anthropic-ai-automate-jobs-pretty-terrible-decade/.

16. Jeran Wittenstein, "AI Can Only Do 5% of Jobs, Says MIT Economist Who Fears Crash," *Bloomberg*, October 2, 2024, https://www.bloomberg.com/news/articles/2024-10-02/ai-can-only-do-5-of-jobs-says-mit-economist-who-fears-crash.

17. "Geoffrey Hinton from University of Toronto Awarded Nobel Prize in Physics," CBC News, October 8, 2024, https://www.cbc.ca/news/science/nobel-prize-physics-2024-1.7344607.

18. Fabrizio Dell'Acqua, Edward McFowland III, Ethan Mollick, Hila Lifshitz-Assaf, Katherine C. Kellogg, Saran Rajendran, et al., "Navigating the Jagged Technological

Frontier: Field Experimental Evidence of the Effects of AI on Knowledge Worker Productivity and Quality," Working Paper No. 24-013 (Harvard Business School, September 2023), https://www.hbs.edu/faculty/Pages/item.aspx?num=64700.

19. Christos Makridis, "Play the Long Game with Human-AI Collaboration," *Gallup Blog*, May 15, 2025, https://www.gallup.com/workplace/660572/play-long-game-human-ai-collaboration.aspx.

Chapter 2

1. Jenna Russell, "Hospitals Are Desperate for Workers. They Might Find Them in High Schools," *New York Times*, January 17, 2024, https://www.nytimes.com/2024/01/17/us/boston-schools-jobs-hospitals-bloomberg.html?searchResultPosition=1.

2. Gwen Moran, "Your AI Hiring Tool May Be Rejecting Qualified Candidates," *Fast Company*, June 10, 2025, https://www.fastcompany.com/91345408/your-ai-hiring-tool-may-be-rejecting-qualified-candidates.

3. Alana Semuels, "You're Not Imagining It, Job Hunting Is Getting Worse," *Time Magazine*, June 14, 2023, https://time.com/6287012/why-finding-job-is-difficult/.

4. See https://gradsoflife.org/skills-first-talent-management/.

5. Matt Sigelman, Joseph Fuller, and Alex Marting, "Skills-Based Hiring: The Long Road from Pronouncements to Practice," Burning Glass Institute, February 14, 2024, https://www.burningglassinstitute.org/research/skills-based-hiring-2024.

6. "Higher Skills for Higher Returns: Embracing A Skills-First Mindset," OneTen, 2023, https://oneten.org/wp-content/uploads/2023/09/OneTen_Embracing_a_Skills-First_Mindset.

7. SHRM Foundation, *The Rise of Alternative Credentials in Hiring* (SHRM Foundation, 2022), https://www.shrm.org/content/dam/en/shrm/about/press-room/The-Rise-Of-Alternative-Credentials-In-Hiring.pdf.

8. Business Roundtable, *Skills Focus: A Guide to Improving Recruitment, Retention, Advancement and Equity* (Business Roundtable, September 2022), https://s3.amazonaws.com/brt.org/A-GuidetoImprovingRecruitmentRetentionAdvancementEquity.September2022.pdf.

9. "Governors Innovate to Spur Skills-Based Hiring," National Governors Association, April 24, 2024, https://www.nga.org/news/commentary/governors-innovate-to-spur-skills-based-hiring/.

10. Elyse Rosenblum, founder and managing partner at Grads of Life, interview with the authors, June 6, 2024.

11. See https://gradsoflife.org/.

12. Grads of Life, *Ten Years of Pioneering Progress in the Skills-First Movement* (Year Up United, October 2024), https://gradsoflife.org/research/ten-years-of-pioneering-progress/.

13. Joseph Fuller and Monjari Raman, *Dismissed by Degrees* (Accenture, Grads of Life, and Harvard Business School, October 2017), https://www.hbs.edu/managing-the-future-of-work/Documents/dismissed-by-degrees.pdf.

14. Grads of Life, *Ten Years of Pioneering Progress*.

15. Alicia Sasser Modestino, Daniel Shoag, and Joshua Ballance, "Upskilling: Do Employers Demand Greater Skills When Workers Are Plentiful?," *Review of Economics and Statistics* 102, no. 4 (2020): 793–805, https://direct.mit.edu/rest/article-abstract/102/4/793/96774/Upskilling-Do-Employers-Demand-Greater-Skill-When?redirectedFrom=fulltext; Alicia Modestino, Mary Burke, Shahriar Sadighi, Rachel B. Sederberg, and Bledi Taska, "No Longer Qualified? Changes in the Supply and Demand for Skills Within Occupations," Research Department Working Paper no. 20-3 (Federal Reserve Bank of Boston, 2020), https://www.bostonfed.org/publications/research-department-working-paper/2020/no-longer-qualified-changes-in-the-supply-and-demand-for-skills-within-occupations.aspx.

16. Sigelman et al., "Skills-Based Hiring."

17. "Impact Measurement Framework," Grads of Life, accessed October 2, 2025, https://gradsoflife.org/impact-measurement-framework/#.

18. Multiple Pathways Initiative, *Skills-Based Internal Mobility Playbook* (Business Roundtable, 2022), https://s3.amazonaws.com/brt.org/Business-RoundtableMultiplePathwaysInitiativeSkills-BasedInternalMobilityPlaybook.pdf?.

19. Lauren Weber, "62% of Americans Lack a College Degree. Can They Solve the Labor Shortage?," *Wall Street Journal*, February 16, 2024, https://www.wsj.com/lifestyle/careers/employers-open-more-doors-to-workers-without-degrees-but-few-are-getting-in-732f1098?mod=author_content_page_4_pos_4.

20. Sigelman et al., "Skills-Based Hiring."

21. Peter Cappelli, *Our Least Important Asset: Why the Relentless Focus on Finance and Accounting Is Bad for Business and Employees* (Oxford University Press, 2023), 49.

22. Lauren Johnson, "Are Employers Losing Out on Valuable Talent Because of Their ATS?," *Human Resource Director*, October 17, 2023, https://www.hcamag.com/us/specialization/hr-technology/are-employers-losing-out-on-valuable-talent-because-of-their-ats/463476.

23. *Ready for Success: A Toolkit for Adopting a Skills Mindset in Employment Practices* (SHRM Foundation, SHRM, and Charles Koch Foundation, May 2023), https://shrm-res.cloudinary.com/image/upload/v1686668654/Skilled%20Credentials/Skilled_Credentials_Toolkit-with_descriptions-v6.pdf.

24. Ashley Whillans and Jeff Polzer, "Applied: Using Behavioral Science to Debias Hiring," Harvard Business School Case 921-046 (Harvard Business School, September 2021), https://www.hbs.edu/faculty/Pages/item.aspx?num=59779.

25. Andrew Chamberlin, "How Long Does It Take to Hire? Interview Duration in 25 Countries," *Glassdoor* (blog), August 9, 2017, https://www.glassdoor.com/blog/time-to-hire-in-25-countries/.

26. Hailey Mensik, "How Companies Like Microsoft, EY and Bank of America Are Hiring More Neurodiverse Staff," WorkLife, April 4, 2024, https://www.worklife.news/talent/neurodiversity-autism-adhd-hiring-interview-microsoft-ey/.

27. Elyse Forbush, director of nutrition and food services at Spaulding Rehabilitation Hospital, interview with the authors, July 8, 2024.

28. See https://spauldingrehab.org/.

29. Kayt Norris, former senior director of growth and innovation at Homebridge, interview with the authors, September 24, 2024. *Note:* Kayt Norris is the primary author of this case study.

30. See https://homebridgeca.org/.

31. See https://www.phinational.org/.

32. See https://ern-usa.com/.

33. See https://www.phinational.org/.

34. Steven Dawson, excerpted from "When the Employer Is the Trainer: Lessons from Cooperative Home Care Associates," *Pinkerton Papers*, no. 5 (June 2017), The Pinkerton Foundation, https://www.thepinkertonfoundation.org/paper_type/job-quality-series. Reprinted with permission. Updated with Adria Powell, president and CEO of Cooperative Home Care Associates, correspondence with the authors, December 10, 2024. Note also that Dawson served as a member of the CHCA corporate board of directors until 2011.

35. See https://www.chcany.org/.

36. Callum Borchers and Lindsay Ellis, "Landing a Job Is All About Who You Know (Again)," *Wall Street Journal*, May 30, 2024, https://www.wsj.com/lifestyle/careers/networking-job-search-c6f06b0c.

37. Borchers and Ellis, "Landing a Job."

38. For more information, see JVS Boston, https://www.jvs-boston.org/for-employers/.

39. Thaddeus Swanek, "New App Helps Companies Fill Roles Using Overlooked Talent Pools," US Chamber of Commerce, April 30, 2024, https://www.uschamber.com/workforce/new-app-helps-companies-fill-roles-using-overlooked-talent-pools.

40. See https://www.blackjobs.com.

41. See https://themomproject.com/.

42. See the Office of Apprenticeship, https://www.apprenticeship.gov/.

43. See JVS Boston, https://masshiredowntownboston.org/trainingtoemployment/jvs-animalcaretech/.

44. Cappelli, *Our Least Important Asset*, 159.

45. "Employee Referral Statistics For 2023," *Atto* (blog), June 19, 2023, https://attotime.com/blog/employee-referral-statistics.

46. Erin White, senior director of Business Roundtable, interview with the authors, August 12, 2024.

47. Joseph B. Fuller, Manjari Raman, Eva Sage-Gavin, and Kristen Hines, *Hidden Workers, Untapped Talent* (Harvard Business School and Accenture, September 2021), 39, https://www.hbs.edu/managing-the-future-of-work/Documents/research/hiddenworkers09032021.pdf.

48. Multiple Pathways Initiative, "Skills-Based Internal Mobility Playbook."

49. Nick Apanius, Tim Steigerwald, Pete Strange, and Rob Verst, senior leadership of Messer Construction, interviews with the authors, 2025, June 5, 2024, and August 5, 2024.

50. See https://www.messer.com/.

51. See "Commitment to Economic Inclusion in Construction Starts at the Top," accessed October 20, 2025, https://www.messer.com/economic-inclusion/.

52. US Bureau of Labor Statistics, "The Employment Situation—April 2025," press release, August 1, 2025, https://www.bls.gov/news.release/pdf/empsit.pdf.

53. Fuller et al., *Hidden Workers, Untapped Talent.*

54. Jerry Rubin and Ayanna Warrington, *Addressing the Labor Shortage in Massachusetts: Engaging Untapped Talent* (Harvard Project on Workforce, September 2023), https://www.pw.hks.harvard.edu/post/addressing-the-labor-shortage-in-massachusetts.

55. Rubin and Warrington, *Addressing the Labor Shortage*.

56. David DeLong, *Hidden Talent: How to Employ Refugees, the Formerly Incarcerated, and People with Disabilities* (Longstone Press, 2024).

57. Katherine Newman and Elizabeth Jacobs, *Moving the Needle* (University of California Press, 2024).

58. US Bureau of Labor Statistics, "Foreign-Born Workers: Labor Force Characteristics—2024," press release, May 20, 2025, https://www.bls.gov/news.release/forbrn.nr0.htm.

59. Alisha Rao, Drishti Pillai, Samantha Artiga, Liz Hamel, Shannon Schumacher, Audrey Kearney, et al., "Five Key Facts About Immigrants with Limited English Proficiency," KFF, March 14, 2024, https://www.kff.org/racial-equity-and-health-policy/issue-brief/five-key-facts-about-immigrants-with-limited-english-proficiency/.

60. "H-1B Program," US Department of Labor, accessed August 12, 2024, https://www.dol.gov/agencies/whd/immigration/h1b.

61. Kate Hooper, "What Role Can Immigration Play in Addressing Current and Future Labor Shortages?," Policy Briefs, Migration Policy Institute, April 2023, https://www.migrationpolicy.org/research/immigration-addressing-labor-shortages.

62. Johan Uvin, Silja Kallenbach, Annalisa Crowe, Catalina González, Navjeet Singh, Jen Vanek, et al., *The Transformation of Adult ESOL Learning: A Practice and Policy Brief* (EdTech Center @ World Education, 2022), https://publications.jsi.com/JSIInternet/Inc/Common/_download_pub.cfm?id=24615&lid=3.

63. "U.S. Resettlement Partners," UNHCR | USA, accessed July 23, 2024, https://www.unhcr.org/us/what-we-do/resettlement-united-states/u-s-resettlement-partners.

64. Emmanuel Owasu, founder and chief executive at ABN, interview with the authors for Rubin and Warrington, *Addressing the Labor Shortage*. Republished with permission. See ABN's website at https://africanbn.org/.

65. See https://africanbn.org/.

66. See https://institute.agefriendly.com/.

67. Andara Kennedy, Anona Neal, and Rose Khattar, "Disabled Workers Saw Record Employment Gains in 2023 but Gaps Remain," Center for American Progress, February 22, 2024, https://www.americanprogress.org/article/disabled-workers-saw-record-employment-gains-in-2023-but-gaps-remain/.

68. Kennedy et al., "Record Employment Gains."

69. "CVS Health Recognized as a 'Best Place to Work for Disability Inclusion,'" CVS Health, July 9, 2018, https://www.cvshealth.com/news/diversity-equity-inclusion/cvs-health-recognized-as-a-best-place-to-work-for-disability.html.

70. Jenny Lyons-Cunha, "In it Together: John Deere's ABLEd ERG Provides a Supportive Space for Its Differently Abled Employees," Built In, March 8, 2023, https://builtin.com/articles/it-together-john-deeres-abled-erg-provides-supportive-space-its-differently-abled-employees.

71. "Empower Through Opportunity," Marriott International, accessed September 9, 2025, https://serve360.marriott.com/empower/.

72. See Listen to Your Mothers, at https://listentoyourmothers.com/.

73. "Labor Force Statistics from the Current Population Survey," US Bureau of Labor Statistics, accessed September 29, 2025, https://www.bls.gov/cps/.

74. "Youth Unemployment," Opportunity Nation, accessed July 13, 2024. https://forumfyi.org/work/on-old/.

75. See Prison Policy Initiative at https://www.prisonpolicy.org/graphs/directlyimpacted2025.html.

76. "Second Chance Employer Profile: Johns Hopkins Medicine," Jails to Jobs, accessed October 2, 2025, https://jailstojobs.org/resources/second-chance-employers-network/johns-hopkins-medicine/; and Jeffrey Korzenik, "How Employers Can Set Formerly Incarcerated Workers Up for Success," *Harvard Business Review*, October 3, 2022, https://hbr.org/2022/10/how-employers-can-set-formerly-incarcerated-workers-up-for-success.

77. Patrick Kline, Evan K. Rose, and Christopher R. Walters, "Systemic Discrimination Among Large U.S. Employers," *Quarterly Journal of Economics* 137, no. 4 (November 2022): 1963–2036, https://doi.org/10.1093/qje/qjac024/.

78. Claire Cain Miller and Josh Katz, "What Researchers Discovered When They Sent 80,000 Fake Résumés to U.S. Jobs," *New York Times*, April 8, 2024, https://www.nytimes.com/2024/04/08/upshot/employment-discrimination-fake-resumes.html.

79. Gabriel Mandujano and Imani Wilkes Burg, Wash Cycle Laundry, interview with the authors, June 23, 2025, https://washcyclelaundry.com/; and Rubin and Warrington, *Addressing the Labor Shortage*, republished with permission.

80. See https://washcyclelaundry.com/.

81. See https://shop.greyston.org/.

82. See https://homeboyindustries.org/.

Chapter 3

1. This case study is authored by Aashi Agarwal and Mehr Pasricha, research assistants at Harvard University's John F. Kennedy School of Government.

2. See https://www.shopmarketbasket.com/.

3. Grant Welker, "Sun Man of the Year Arthur T. Demoulas Puts Workers, Customers Ahead of Profits," *Lowell Sun*, January 14, 2014, updated July 12, 2019, https://www.lowellsun.com/2014/01/14/sun-man-of-the-year-arthur-t-demoulas-puts-workers-customers-ahead-of-profits/.

4. Adam Vaccaro, "Wages Not All That's at Stake for Part-Time Market Basket Workers," *Boston.com*, August 7, 2014, https://www.boston.com/news/business/2014/08/07/wages-not-all-thats-at-stake-for-part-time-market-basket-workers/.

5. Grant Welker, "Before You Know It, You're in It for Life," *Lowell Sun*, updated July 12, 2019. https://www.lowellsun.com/2014/08/09/before-you-know-it-youre-in-it-for-life/.

6. Julia Wong, "At Market Basket, the Benevolent Boss Is Back. Should We Cheer?" *In These Times*, August 30, 2014, https://inthesetimes.com/article/at-market-basket-the-benevolent-boss-is-back-should-we-cheer.

7. Soyhan Egitim, "The Market Basket Case Revisited: Community Empowerment Through Leaderful Organizational Culture," *Journal of Leadership Studies* 17, no. 1 (Spring 2023): 51–56, https://doi.org/10.1002/JLS.21844.

8. Joey DeGrado, "The Tiny Grocery Chain That Beats Inflation Like No Other," Food Republic, March 16, 2024, https://www.foodrepublic.com/1535151/market-basket-grocery-chain-beats-inflation/.

9. Zeynep Ton, Thomas A. Kochan, and Cate Reavis, *"We Are Market Basket,"* MIT Sloan School, case study 14-160, March 23, 2015, https://mitsloan.mit.edu/sites/default/files/2020-03/We%20Are%20Market%20Basket.IC_.pdf.

10. Daniel Korschun and Grant Welker, *We Are Market Basket* (HarperCollins Leadership, 2022), 89.

11. Korschun and Welker, *We Are Market Basket*, 178.

12. Bailey Allen, "Read Market Basket's Complaint Against Fired CEO Arthur T. Demoulas," *USA Today Network*, September 12, 2025, https://www.seacoastonline.com/story/business/2025/09/12/read-action-against-arthur-t-demoulas-in-delaware-court-of-chancery-market-basket/86109634007/.

13. Rick Wartzman, *The End of Loyalty: The Rise and Fall of Good Jobs in America*, reprint edition (PublicAffairs, 2018).

14. "The Productivity–Pay Gap," Economic Policy Institute (EPI), April 2025, updated September 3, 2025, https://www.epi.org/productivity-pay-gap/.

15. "Productivity–Pay Gap."

16. Investopedia Team, "Rule 10b-18 Definition and How Compliance Works," Investopedia, January 10, 2021, https://www.investopedia.com/terms/r/rule10b18.asp.

17. Abigail Tierney, "Real and Nominal Value of the Federal Minimum Wage in the United States from 1938 to 2024," Statistica, July 26, 2024, https://www.statista.com/statistics/1065466/real-nominal-value-minimum-wage-us/.

18. "Average Hourly Earnings of Production and Nonsupervisory Employees, Total Private," Federal Reserve Bank of St. Louis, accessed November 1, 2024, https://fred.stlouisfed.org/series/AHETPI.

19. Lawrence Mishel, Lynn Rhinehart, and Lane Windham, "Explaining the Erosion of Private-Sector Unions," Economic Policy Institute, November 18, 2020, https://www.epi.org/unequalpower/publications/private-sector-unions-corporate-legal-erosion/.

20. Jeanne Sahadi, "Traditional Pension Plans Are Pretty Rare. But Here's Who Still Has Them and How They Work," CNN, September 7, 2023, https://www.cnn.com/2023/09/07/success/pensions-retirement-savings-explained#.

21. "New Single-Family Home Prices: 1964–Present," Bureau of the Census, Department of Commerce, and Office of Policy Development and Research, Department of Housing and Urban Development, accessed September 30, 2025, https://www.huduser.gov/periodicals/ushmc/winter2001/histdat08.htm.

22. "Average Hourly Earnings of Production and Nonsupervisory Employees, Total Private," Federal Reserve Bank of St. Louis, updated September 5, 2025, https://fred.stlouisfed.org/series/AHETPI.

23. Redfin, "United States Housing Market," accessed September 30, 2025, https://www.redfin.com/us-housing-market.

24. David Weil, *The Fissured Workplace: Why Work Became So Bad for So Many and What Can Be Done to Improve It* (Harvard University Press, 2014).

25. *2023–24 SHRM State of the Workplace Report* (SHRM, 2024), 8, https://www.shrm.org/content/dam/en/shrm/research/2023-2024-State-of-the-Workplace-Report.pdf.

26. "Employee Engagement," Gallup, accessed December 23, 2024, https://www.gallup.com/394373/indicator-employee-engagement.aspx#:~:text=I.

27. "Employee Retention & Attraction," Gallup, accessed December 23, 2024, https://www.gallup.com/467702/indicator-employee-retention-attraction.aspx.

28. Jim Harter, "Leaders: Ignore Employee Wellbeing At Your Own Risk," Gallup, July 6, 2023, https://www.gallup.com/workplace/507974/leaders-ignore-employee-wellbeing-own-risk.aspx#.

29. Corey Tatel and Ben Wigert, "42% of Employee Turnover Is Preventable but Often Ignored," Gallup, July 9, 2024, https://www.gallup.com/workplace/646538/employee-turnover-preventable-often-ignored.aspx.

30. Emily Guendelsberger, *On the Clock: What Low-Wage Work Did to Me and How It Drives America Insane* (Little, Brown and Company, 2019).

31. Dr. Zeynep Ton, professor of the practice at MIT Sloan School of Management and president of Good Jobs Institute, interview with the authors, October 11, 2024.

32. Christine Trayner, former head of recruitment at Little Sprouts, interview with the authors, March 14, 2024.

33. See https://littlesprouts.com/.

34. Kristin Butcher, Elizabeth Kepner, Kelli Marquardt, and Brianna Smith, "The Labor Market for Childcare Workers," *Chicago Fed Insights*, June 2024, https://www.chicagofed.org/publications/chicago-fed-insights/2024/childcare-labor-market.

35. Butcher et al., "Labor Market for Childcare Workers."

36. See https://www.neighborhoodvillages.org/.

37. Drew Greenblatt, CEO of Marlin Steel, interview with the authors, August 26, 2024.

38. See https://www.marlinwire.com/.

39. Jack Stack, president and CEO of SRC Holdings Corp., interview with the authors, November 19, 2024.

40. Scott Koloms, CEO of FMS, interview with the authors, August 2, 2024.

41. Michael Elsas, retired CEO/president of Cooperative Home Care Associates, interview with the authors, August 26, 2024.

42. See https://www.chcany.org/.

43. Scott Koloms, CEO of FMS, interview with the authors, August 2, 2024.

44. See https://www.lagustascafe.com/.

45. See https://softerpowersweets.com/.

46. Lagusta Yearwood, founder of Lagusta's Cafe and Softer Power Sweets, interview with the authors, August 30, 2024.

47. Paul Neumann, retired CEO and current board member of UW Solutions, interview with the authors, August 27, 2024. Note that this case study also draws on a previous case study authored by Steven Dawson, published by The National Fund for Workforce Solutions, May 4, 2017. See https://nationalfund.org/our-resources/publications/universal-woods-business-logic-of-trust/.

48. See https://www.uwsolutions.com/.

49. "Good Companies/Good Jobs," Aspen Institute, accessed September 30, 2025, https://www.aspeninstitute.org/programs/good-companies-good-jobs/.

50. "Good Jobs Champions Group: Statement on Good Jobs," Aspen Institute, accessed September 30, 2025, https://www.aspeninstitute.org/programs/good-jobs-champions-group/.

51. Daniel H. Pink, *Drive: The Surprising Truth About What Motivates Us* (Riverhead Books, 2011), 10.

52. See https://www.shrm.org/home.

53. Curt Lyon and Julie Menter, *Investing in Employee Ownership: Overview for Mission-Oriented Investors* (Transform Finance, August 2024), https://www.transformfinance.org/investing-in-employee-ownership-report.

54. Joseph Blasi and Douglas Kruse, "Employee Ownership and ESOPS: Recent Research on Benefits and Challenges" (Aspen Institute, 2024), https://policycommons.net/artifacts/12039579/employee-ownership-and-esops/12933835/.

55. Nick Apanius, Tim Steigerwald, Pete Strange, and Rob Verst, senior leadership of Messer Construction, interviews with the authors, June 5, 2024, and August 5, 2024.

56. See https://www.messer.com/.

57. Blasi and Kruse, *Employee Ownership and ESOPS.*

58. *2023 Worker Cooperative State of the Sector Report* (Democracy at Work Institute and United States Federation of Worker Cooperatives, 2023), https://democracy.institute.coop/sots2023.

59. See https://www.purposeowned.com/.

60. See https://ownershipworks.org/.

61. Lori Butterfield, "Tackling the Wealth Gap: KKR's Pete Stavros and a New Employee Ownership Model," Stanford Graduate School of Business, Stanford University, May 17, 2023, https://casi.stanford.edu/news/tackling-wealth-gap-kkrs-pete-stavros-and-new-employee-ownership-model.

62. See https://ownershipworks.org/how-we-help/.

63. See https://ownershipworks.org/companies-and-case-studies/.

64. See https://expandingesops.com/.

65. Steve Gelsi, "KKR's Pete Stavros Launches Group Promoting Stock Ownership for Employees," Morningstar, September 24, 2024, https://www.morningstar.com/news/marketwatch/2024092461/kkrs-pete-stavros-launches-group-promoting-stock-ownership-for-employees.

66. John Abrams, *From Founder to Future: A Business Roadmap to Impact, Longevity, and Employee Ownership* (Berrett-Koehler Publishers, 2025).

67. See https://deansbeans.com/.

68. See https://snowrivercustom.com/.

69. For ESOPs, see the Institute for the Study of Employee Ownership and Profit Sharing at the Rutgers School of Management and Labor Relations, https://smlr.rutgers.edu/faculty-research-engagement/institute-study-employee-ownership-and-profit-sharing; for worker cooperatives, see the Democracy at Work Institute, https://institute.coop; and for perpetual purpose trusts, see Purpose Owned, https://www.purposeowned.com/.

70. Dr. Alan Robinson, professor at the University of Massachusetts, interview with the authors, August 30, 2024.

71. Alan G. Robinson and Dean M. Schroeder, *The Idea-Driven Organization: Unlocking the Power in Bottom-Up Ideas*, reprint edition (Berrett-Koehler Publishers, 2020).

72. Alan G. Robinson, "Speaking Topics of Bestselling Author Alan G. Robinson," https://alanrobinson.com/wp-content/thesis/skins/mobile-first/images/alan_robinson_one_sheet.pdf?utm.

73. Alan G. Robinson and Dean M. Schroeder, "How to Unlock Employee Ideas to Power Your Organization," *Change This* (blog), Porchlight, June 11, 2014, https://www.porchlightbooks.com/blog/changethis/2014/how-to-unlock-employee-ideas-to-power-your-organization.

74. Robinson and Schroeder, "How to Unlock Employee Ideas to Power Your Organization."

75. Robinson and Schroeder, "How to Unlock Employee Ideas to Power Your Organization," 12.

76. Robinson and Schroeder, "How to Unlock Employee Ideas to Power Your Organization," 12.

77. "The Q12®: The World's Leading Employee Engagement Survey," Gallup Workplace, accessed September 30, 2025, https://www.gallup.com/q12-employee-engagement-survey/.

78. Rajendra S. Sisodia, David B. Wolfe, and Jagdish N. Sheth, *Firms of Endearment: How World-Class Companies Profit from Passion and Purpose* (Wharton School Publishing, 2007).

79. See https://www.conference-board.org/us.

80. Ton, interview with the authors.

81. Zeynep Ton, "The Case for Good Jobs—and Why They're Good for Business Too," TED2024, April 2024, https://www.ted.com/talks/zeynep_ton_the_case_for_good_jobs_and_why_they_re_good_for_business_too?subtitle=en.

82. See https://goodjobsinstitute.org/.

83. Ari Weinzweig, cofounder of Zingerman's Community of Businesses, interview with the authors, September 3, 2024.

84. See https://www.zingermanscommunity.com/.

85. Ari Weinzweig, "Sharing the Next Big Step in Zingerman's History—a Perpetual Purpose Trust," *Zingerman's Community of Businesses* (blog), February 2, 2023, https://www.zingermanscommunity.com/2023/02/sharing-the-next-big-step-in-zingermans-history-perpetual-purpose-trust/.

86. Ari Weinzweig, *A Revolution of Dignity in the Twenty-First Century Workplace* (Zingerman's Press, 2024), https://www.zingermanspress.com/product/a-revolution-of-dignity-in-the-twenty-first-century-workplace/.

87. See https://www.zingtrain.com/.

88. Mike Ganino, host, *Mike Drop Moment*, podcast, episode 44, "Transformational Training with Baggie Bayless from ZingTrain," Spotify, January 18, 2023, https://open.spotify.com/episode/49VEt6wIQzFbNGMa4Oxa2N.

89. Ganino, *Mike Drop Moment.*

90. "Zingerman's 2032 Vision," *ZingTrain* (blog), accessed September 30, 2025, https://www.zingtrain.com/blog/zingermans-2032-vision/.

91. Jack Stack, president and CEO of SRC Holdings Corp., interview with the authors, November 19, 2024.

92. See https://www.srcholdings.com/.

93. "The Smartest Strategist in America," *Inc. Magazine*, December 2011.

94. SRC Holdings Website, accessed September 30, 2025, https://www.srcholdings.com/about.

95. See https://www.greatgame.com/.

96. See https://www.greatgame.com/business-coaching.

Chapter 4

1. Tom Weber, executive director of the Massachusetts Business Coalition for Early Childhood Education, interview with the authors, July 1, 2024.

2. See https://www.businessleadersunited.org/ and https://nationalskillscoalition.org/.

3. See https://www.businessroundtable.org/policy-perspectives/building-americas-ever-ready-workforce.

4. Dane Linn, senior vice president of corporate initiatives, immigration, and Erin White, senior director of corporate initiatives, at Business Roundtable, interview with the authors, August 7, 2024. For more information, see https://www.businessroundtable.org/policy-perspectives/building-americas-ever-ready-workforce/workforce-development.

5. Ted Abernathy, Greg Payne, and Economic Leadership, *Workforce: A Throttle on American Growth* (National Association of State Chambers, 2022), https://cosc.memberclicks.net/assets/NASC-Report-8.30.22%20%28Final%20with%20all%20edits%29.pdf.

6. "Opportunity Summit: Investing in American Jobs," Walmart, Washington, DC, April 24, 2024, https://corporate.walmart.com/content/dam/corporate/documents/suppliers/investing-in-american-jobs/events/opportunity-summit/Opportunity_Summit_2024_Blueprint.pdf.

7. Alexander Bick, Victoria Gregory, and Oksana Leukhina, "How Childcare Impacts Parents' Labor Force Participation," *On the Economy Blog*, Federal Reserve Bank of St. Louis, July 10, 2024, https://www.stlouisfed.org/on-the-economy/2023/jul/how-child-care-impacts-parents-labor-force-participation.

8. Bick et al., "Parents' Labor Force Participation."

9. Stephanie Ferguson Melhorn, "Understanding America's Labor Shortage: The Impact of Scarce and Costly Childcare," US Chamber of Commerce, June 26, 2024, https://www.uschamber.com/workforce/understanding-americas-labor-shortage-the-scarce-and-costly-childcare-issue; and *2024: The Future of Benefits* (Care.com, 2024), https://www.care.com/business/reports/2024-future-of-benefits-report/.

10. "Incentivizing Employer-Supported Child Care in Massachusetts," Massachusetts Taxpayers Foundation, July 13, 2023, https://www.masstaxpayers.org/sites/default/files/publications/2023-07/Employer%20Supported%20Care%20Paper%20Final_0.pdf.

11. US Bureau of Labor Statistics, "Employee Benefits in the United States Summary," press release, September 19, 2024, https://www.bls.gov/news.release/ebs2.nr0.htm.

12. REBNY Staff, "Business, Labor and Nonprofit Groups Launch New Coalition to Increase Child Care Access for NYC Families," Real Estate Board of New York, February 21, 2024, https://www.rebny.com/press-release/business-labor-and-nonprofit-groups-launch-new-coalition-to-increase-child/.

13. REBNY Staff, "Access for NYC Families."

14. Jay Lindsay, "Can Employers Play a Larger Role in Solving the Nation's Childcare Crisis?," Federal Reserve Bank of Boston, March 20, 2024, https://www.bostonfed.org/news-and-events/news/2024/03/child-care-crisis-getting-employers-more-involved-sarah-savage-boston-fed.aspx.

15. Tom Weber, executive director of the Massachusetts Business Coalition for Early Childhood Education, interview with the authors, July 1, 2025.

16. See https://www.maroundtable.com/mbcece/.

17. Aaron Shroyer and Veronica Gaitán, "Four Reasons Why Employers Should Care About Housing," Housing Matters, Urban Institute, September 11, 2019, https://housingmatters.urban.org/articles/four-reasons-why-employers-should-care-about-housing.

18. Shroyer and Gaitán, "Employers Should Care About Housing."

19. Meg Cunningham, "Amazon Employees Can Now Use Their Company Stock to Secure Home Loans," Investopedia, February 28, 2023, https://www.investopedia.com/amazon-employees-stock-home-loans-7152612.

20. Edward L. Glaeser and Atta Tarki, "What Employers Can Do to Address High Housing Costs," *Harvard Business Review*, March 14, 2023, https://hbr.org/2023/03/what-employers-can-do-to-address-high-housing-costs.

21. Jessica McDermott and Tyler Work, "Affordable Housing in the Upper Valley," PRS Policy Brief 1819-09 (Nelson A. Rockefeller Center at Dartmouth College, April 24, 2019), https://rockefeller.dartmouth.edu/sites/rockefeller.prod/files/prs_chmc_report_053119.pdf.

22. Nathan Ho, "Advocating for Affordable Housing in the Bay Area," Silicon Valley Leadership Group, May 15, 2019, https://www.svlg.org/advocating-for-affordable-housing-in-the-bay-area/.

23. David Juvet, Kirsten Koch, and Rick Fabrizio, "2024 Legislative Agenda," BIA, accessed September 11, 2024, https://www.biaofnh.com/assets/pdf/2024+Public+Policy+Priorities+--+FINAL/.

24. John Chesto, "As Housing Battles Brew, Business Leaders Join the Push to Build More," *Boston Globe*, October 5, 2024, https://www.bostonglobe.com/2024/10/05/business/greater-boston-housing-business-leaders/.

25. "The Impact of Public Transit on the Workforce and Local Economies in the U.S.," Modeshift, June 3, 2024, https://www.modeshift.com/thimpact-of-public-transit-on-the-workforce-and-local-economies-us/.

26. Joseph Mengedoth, "Transportation Access as a Barrier to Work," *Econ Focus*, Federal Reserve Bank of Richmond, December 19, 2023, https://www.richmondfed.org/publications/research/econ_focus/2023/q4_district_digest#.

27. Economic Development Research Group, *Economic Impact of Public Transportation Investment: 2020 Update* (American Public Transportation Association, April 2020), https://www.apta.com/wp-content/uploads/APTA-Economic-Impact-Public-Transit-2020.pdf.

28. Nina R. Joyce, Melissa R. Pfeiffer, Andrew R. Zullo, Jasjit Ahluwalia, and Allison E. Curry, "Individual and Geographic Variation in Driver's License Suspensions: Evidence of Disparities by Race, Ethnicity and Income," *Journal of Transport & Health* 19 (December 2020), https://doi.org/10.1016/j.jth.2020.100933.

29. See https://facilitiesmgmt.com/about/.

30. Taylor Dolven, "Worcester Public Transport Will Remain Fare-Free for a Fifth Year," *Boston Globe*, April 18, 2024, https://www.bostonglobe.com/2024/04/18/metro/worcester-fare-free-fifth-year/.

31. Dolven, "Worcester Public Transport."

32. See https://www.getdowntown.org/gopass.

33. Paul Kiernan, "How Immigration Remade the U.S. Labor Force," *Wall Street Journal*, September 4, 2024, https://www.wsj.com/economy/how-immigration-remade-the-u-s-labor-force-716c18ee.

34. See https://www.businessroundtable.org/policy-perspectives/immigration.

35. "Topics / Immigration," U.S. Chamber of Commerce, accessed August 15, 2024, https://www.uschamber.com/immigration.

36. "Upwardly Global Applauds Introduction of 'Welcome Back to the Health Care Workforce Act' Enabling Immigrants to Refuel Healthcare Workforce," Upwardly Global, April 12, 2024, https://www.upwardlyglobal.org/news/news/upwardly-global-welcome-back-to-the-health-care-workforce-act/.

37. See https://www.americanimmigrationcouncil.org/state-local-initiatives/global-talent-chamber-network/.

38. See https://www.ohcompact.org/.

39. Gabriela Parra, "Two in Three Americans Support the Bipartisan Immigration Deal," Navigator, February 29, 2024, https://navigatorresearch.org/two-in-three-americans-support-the-bipartisan-immigration-deal/.

Chapter 5

1. Angela Jackson, Kyle Abert, Olivia Gunther, Ashley Yuan, and Guy Berger, *The Competitive Advantage of the Win-Win Workplace* (Future Forward Institute, October 2024), https://www.futureforward.institute/win-win-workplace-report.

2. John Hamilton, business consultant, interview with the authors, July 26, 2024.

3. See https://communityloanfund.org/.

4. Note that this analysis on resistance to change draws on a previous case study authored by Steven Dawson, published by The National Fund for Workforce Solutions, June 9, 2020. See https://nationalfund.org/our-resources/publications/appreciating-employer-resistance-to-job-design-changes/.

5. Simon Rabinovitch and Henry Curr, "The American Economy Has Left Other Rich Countries in the Dust," *The Economist*, October 14, 2024, https://www.economist.com/special-report/2024/10/14/the-american-economy-has-left-other-rich-countries-in-the-dust.

6. Peter Cappelli, *Our Least Important Asset: Why the Relentless Focus on Finance and Accounting Is Bad for Business and Employees* (Oxford University Press, 2023).

7. See the Louisiana licensing requirements at the Best Cosmetology Schools Directory, https://bestcosmetologyschools.org/state-requirements/louisiana/.

8. See the requirements at the Arizona State Board of Massage Therapy site, https://massagetherapy.az.gov/applications.

9. "Nurse Delegation," AARP, accessed September 30, 2025, https://ltsschoices.aarp.org/scorecard-report/2023/dimensions-and-indicators/nurse-delegation.

10. Labor Management Relations Act of 1947, § 302, 29 U.S.C. § 186 (1947), https://www.justice.gov/archives/jm/criminal-resource-manual-2413-outline-29-usc-186-taft-hartley-act-sec-302.

11. Adam Galinsky, "When You're in Charge, Your Whisper May Feel Like a Shout," *New York Times*, August 15, 2015, https://www.nytimes.com/2015/08/16/jobs/when-youre-in-charge-your-whisper-may-feel-like-a-shout.html?smid=url-share.

12. Daniel H. Pink, *Drive: The Surprising Truth About What Motivates Us* (Riverhead Books, 2011), 203.

13. Katie Moussouris, founder and CEO of Luta Security, interview with the authors, August 8, 2024.

14. See https://www.lutasecurity.com/.

15. See https://www.payequitynowfoundation.org/.

16. David L. Cooperrider and Suresh Srivastva, "Appreciative Inquiry in Organizational Life," Research in Organizational Change and Development 1 (1987): 129–169, https://www.researchgate.net/publication/265225217_Appreciative_Inquiry_in_Organizational_Life.

17. Scott Koloms, CEO of FMS, interview with the authors, August 2, 2024.

18. Robert Slater, *Jack Welch and the GE Way: Management Insights and Leadership Secrets of the Legendary CEO* (McGraw-Hill, 1999).

19. Jessica Bruder, *Nomadland: Surviving America in the Twenty-First Century* (W. W. Norton & Company, 2017), 90–110.

20. Pete Strange, chairman emeritus of Messer Construction, interview with the authors, June 25, 2024.

21. "Employee Training Statistics & Data in the U.S. (2024/2025)," HIGH 5 TEST, accessed September 30, 2025, https://high5test.com/employee-training-statistics/.

22. Jeffrey Pfeffer, *The Human Equation: Building Profits by Putting People First* (Harvard Business School Press, 1980).

23. Heather McGhee, *The Sum of Us: What Racism Costs Everyone and How We Can Prosper Together* (One World, 2021).

24. Frank Dobbin and Alexandra Kalev, *Getting to Diversity: What Works and What Doesn't* (Harvard University Press, 2022).

Chapter 6

1. Moise Duge, founding CEO at Jaspen Group, interview with the authors, July 3, 2024.

2. Pete Strange, chairman emeritus of Messer Construction, interview with the authors, June 25, 2024.

3. Ale' Mendoza, director of human resources at Optimax, interview with the authors, October 8, 2024.

4. Robert Schwartz and Rachel Lipson, *America's Hidden Economic Engines: How Community Colleges Can Drive Shared Prosperity* (Harvard Education Press, 2023).

5. Schwartz and Lipson, *America's Hidden Economic Engines*.

6. Schwartz and Lipson.

7. Ale' Mendoza, director of human resources at Optimax, interview with the authors, October 8, 2024.

8. See https://www.optimaxsi.com/.

9. See https://www.monroecc.edu/.

10. See https://www.flcc.edu/.

11. See https://www.messer.com/.

12. See https://www.nationalcivicleague.org/promising-practices/partnership-for-inclusive-employment-and-career-excellence-piece/.

13. See https./ /www.ptechnyc.org.

14. "P-TECH 9–14 Schools: An Impact, Implementation and Cost Study," Institute of Education Sciences, accessed October 2, 2025, https://ies.ed.gov/use-work/awards/p-tech-9-14-schools-impact-implementation-and-cost-study#.

15. Jerry Rubin and Rouguiatou Diallo, "The Catapult Papers: Essays on the Future of Workforce Development," Boston Foundation, March 7, 2019, https://www.tbf.org/news-and-insights/videos/2019/mar/catapult-forum-20190307.

16. Kira Khazatsky, president and CEO of JVS Boston, interview with the authors, July 10, 2024. Coauthor Jerry Rubin was the president and CEO of JVS Boston from 2007 through 2022.

17. See https://www.jvs-boston.org/.

18. See https://jvs.gibbsss.com/survey/VolejRejNm.

19. See https://nationalfund.org/.

20. See https://chicagoworkforcefunders.org/.

21. See https://caracollective.org/cara-plus/.

22. See https://civicworks.com/.

23. See https://jvs.org/.

24. See https://www.phinational.org/. Coauthor Steven L. Dawson was the president of PHI from 1991 through 2012.

25. Plineo Ayala, CEO of Per Scholas, interview with the authors, September 5, 2024.

26. See https://perscholas.org/.

27. Lee Adams, Jing Cai, Janelle Grant, Brad J. Hershbein, and Bridget F. Timmeney, *Evaluation of Per Scholas as an Employee Recruiting Tool for Businesses* (W. E. Upjohn Institute for Employment Research, September 27, 2019), https://research.upjohn.org/reports/241/.

28. Roy E. Bahat, Thomas A. Kochan, and Liba Wenig Rubenstein, "The Labor-Savvy Leader," *Harvard Business Review*, July–August 2023, https://hbr.org/2023/07/the-labor-savvy-leader.

29. "Labor Unions," Gallup, accessed August 1, 2024, https://news.gallup.com/poll/12751/labor-unions.aspx.

30. Rick Wartzman, *The End of Loyalty: The Rise and Fall of Good Jobs in America*, reprint edition (PublicAffairs, 2018).

31. See https://www.bfri.org/.

32. See Culinary Academy Las Vegas, https://www.theculinaryacademy.org/.

33. See https://besthtc.org/.

34. Aisha Necoechea, executive director of BEST, interview with the authors, October 29, 2024.

35. See https://www.local26.org/.

36. Jon Cresslin, managing director of the Hilton Boston Park Plaza, quote provided to authors by BEST with permission, October 29, 2024.

37. See https://1199ctraining.org/.

38. See SEIU Healthcare 1199NW Multi-Employer Training Fund, https://healthcareerfund.org/.

39. David Deming, Alexis Gable, Rachel Lipson, and Arkādijs Zvaigzne, *Navigating Public Job Training* (Project on Workforce, March 8, 2023), https://www.pw.hks.harvard.edu/post/publicjobtraining.

40. See https://www.nist.gov/mep.

Conclusion

1. Michael Abrashoff, *It's Your Ship: Management Techniques from the Best Damn Ship in the Navy* (Grand Central Publishing, 2007).

2. Abrashoff, *It's Your Ship: Management Techniques from the Best Damn Ship in the Navy* (Grand Central Publishing, 2007), chap. 4.

3. Peggy Powell, senior advisor at PHI, interview with the authors, April 9, 2025.

Index

The letter *f* following a page number denotes a figure.